AFGHANS

FOR ALL SEASONS · BOOK 2

Explore the beauty of all four seasons with this superb collection of crocheted afghans! We've gathered more than 50 of our favorite designs to liven up your home year-round. You'll find projects as fresh and colorful as the blooms of spring, and throws reminiscent of warm summer days. In fall, the cozy afghans speak of changing leaves and harvest time while they invite you to cuddle up by the fire. Winter brings rich and hearty throws for chasing away evening chills. At Leisure Arts, we know what crocheters like — beautiful projects and lots of them! Whether you've spent years perfecting your crochet skills or you're just getting started, there's something for you in this exciting volume of wonderful wraps.

As always, Afghans For All Seasons *will help you every step of the way with materials lists, easy-to-follow instructions, and placement diagrams, so it's easy to whip up something special for anyone in the family. Make a masculine throw for Dad and a lacy one for Mom, or choose from the many adorable afghans just for little ones. We simply can't think of a better way to share the splendor of each passing season!*

LEISURE ARTS, INC. and OXMOOR HOUSE, INC.

EDITORIAL STAFF

Vice President and Editor-at-Large: Anne Van Wagner Childs
Vice President and Editor-in-Chief: Sandra Graham Case
Director of Designer Relations: Debra Nettles
Editorial Director: Susan Frantz Wiles
Publications Director: Susan White Sullivan
Creative Art Director: Gloria Bearden
Photography Director: Karen Hall
Art Operations Director: Jeff Curtis

PRODUCTION
Managing Editor: Valesha M. Kirksey
Senior Technical Editor: Cathy Hardy
Instructional Editors: Susan Ackerman Carter and Sue Galucki

EDITORIAL
Managing Editor: Suzie Puckett
Senior Associate Editor: Stacey Robertson Marshall
Associate Editor: Susan McManus Johnson

ART
Art Director: Mark Hawkins
Senior Production Artist and Color Technician: Mark Potter
Production Artist: Faith Lloyd
Staff Photographer: Russell Ganser
Photostylists: Sondra Daniel, Tiffany Huffman, and Janna Laughlin
Publishing Systems Administrator: Becky Riddle
Publishing Systems Assistants: Myra S. Means and Chris Wertenberger

PROMOTIONS
Associate Editor: Steve Cooper
Designer: Dale Rowett
Graphic Artist: Deborah Kelly

BUSINESS STAFF

Publisher: Rick Barton
Vice President, Finance: Tom Siebenmorgen
**Director of Corporate Planning
    and Development:** Laticia Mull Cornett
Vice President, Retail Marketing: Bob Humphrey
Vice President, Sales: Ray Shelgosh
Vice President, National Accounts: Pam Stebbins
Retail Marketing Director: Margaret Sweetin
Vice President, Operations: Jim Dittrich
Comptroller, Operations: Rob Thieme
Retail Customer Service Manager: Wanda Price
Print Production Manager: Fred F. Pruss

Afghans For All Seasons, Book 2
Published by Leisure Arts, Inc., and Oxmoor House, Inc.

Hardcover ISBN 1-57486-212-X
Softcover ISBN 1-57486-213-8

TABLE OF CONTENTS

SPRING

When the trees begin to show new life and flowers unveil
their beautiful blooms, it's a sure sign that spring has
arrived. The vivid colors and tantalizing smells delight
our senses and inspire our imaginations. Reminiscent of
this stunning season, the afghans in this collection feature
pretty floral designs, intricate patterns, and refreshing
color schemes just right for cool spring days.

GENTLE RAINDROPS

Snuggle into this soothing wrap to watch the renewing rains of spring. The teardrop pattern is created with long double crochets, and wispy fringe finishes the edges.

Finished Size: 48$^{1}/_{2}$ " x 66$^{1}/_{2}$ "

MATERIALS
Worsted Weight Yarn:
Green - 29$^{1}/_{2}$ ounces, (840 grams, 2,025 yards)
Lt Green - 28$^{1}/_{2}$ ounces,
(810 grams, 1,955 yards)
Crochet hook, size H (5.00 mm) **or** size needed for gauge

GAUGE: In pattern, 14 sts and 12 rows = 4";
2 repeats = 3$^{1}/_{2}$ "

Gauge Swatch: 5"w x 4"h
Ch 19 **loosely**.
Work same as Afghan for 12 rows.

STITCH GUIDE

LONG DOUBLE CROCHET *(abbreviated LDC)*
YO, working **around** previous 2 rows *(Fig. 16, page 141)*, insert hook in skipped dc 2 rows **below**, YO and pull up a loop even with last sc made, (YO and draw through 2 loops on hook) twice *(Fig. 9, page 139)*.

Note: Each row is worked across length of Afghan. When joining yarn and finishing off, leave an 11" length to be worked into fringe.

AFGHAN
With Green, ch 229 **loosely**.
Row 1 (Right side): Working in back ridges of beginning ch *(Fig. 2b, page 137)*, dc in fourth ch from hook **(3 skipped chs count as first dc)** and in next 3 chs, ★ ch 1, skip next ch, dc in next 5 chs; repeat from ★ across; finish off: 190 dc and 37 ch-1 sps.
Note: Mark Row 1 as **right** side.

Row 2: With **wrong** side facing, join Lt Green with sc in first dc *(see Joining With Sc, page 140)*; sc in next dc, ch 1, skip next dc, sc in next 2 dc, ★ YO, working around previous row, insert hook in back ridge of beginning ch **below** next ch, YO and pull up a loop even with last sc made, (YO and draw through 2 loops on hook) twice, sc in next 2 dc, ch 1, skip next dc, sc in next 2 dc; repeat from ★ across; finish off: 189 sts and 38 ch-1 sps.
Row 3: With **right** side facing, join Lt Green with slip st in first sc; ch 3 **(counts as first dc, now and throughout)**, dc in next sc, ★ ch 1, skip next ch-1 sp, dc in next 5 sts; repeat from ★ across to last ch-1 sp, ch 1, skip last ch-1 sp, dc in last 2 sc; finish off.
Row 4: With **wrong** side facing, join Green with sc in first dc; sc in next dc, work LDC, sc in next 2 dc, ★ ch 1, skip next dc, sc in next 2 dc, work LDC, sc in next 2 dc; repeat from ★ across; finish off: 190 sts and 37 ch-1 sps.
Row 5: With **right** side facing, join Green with slip st in first sc; ch 3, dc in next 4 sts, ★ ch 1, skip next ch-1 sp, dc in next 5 sts; repeat from ★ across; finish off.
Row 6: With **wrong** side facing, join Lt Green with sc in first dc; sc in next dc, ch 1, skip next dc, sc in next 2 dc, ★ work LDC, sc in next 2 dc, ch 1, skip next dc, sc in next 2 dc; repeat from ★ across; finish off: 189 sts and 38 ch-1 sps.
Repeat Rows 3-6 until Afghan measures approximately 47$^{1}/_{2}$ " from beginning ch, ending by working Row 3.
Next Row: With **wrong** side facing, join Green with sc in first dc; sc in next dc, work LDC, (sc in next 5 dc, work LDC) across to last 2 dc, sc in last 2 dc; finish off: 227 sts.
Last Row: With **right** side facing, join Green with slip st in first sc; ch 3, dc in next sc and in each st across; finish off.

Using photo as a guide for placement and holding 5 strands of corresponding color yarn together, add fringe in end of rows across short edges of Afghan *(Figs. 22b & d, page 142)*.

VINTAGE LACE

Soft, cream-colored yarn gives this beauty of an afghan its timeless appeal.
The body works up quickly in an old-fashioned herringbone pattern,
while the lacy edging adds a touch of Victorian style.

Finished Size: 48¹/₂ " x 68"

MATERIALS

Worsted Weight Yarn:
   46 ounces, (1,310 grams, 2,600 yards)
Crochet hook, size I (5.50 mm) **or** size needed
   for gauge

GAUGE: One repeat (from point to point) = 4";
   5 rows = 2¹/₂ "

Gauge Swatch: 7¹/₄ "w x 4"h
Ch 32 **loosely.**
Work same as Afghan Body for 6 rows.
Finish off.

STITCH GUIDE

> **DECREASE** (uses next 4 ch-3 sps)
> ★ YO, insert hook in **next** ch-3 sp, YO and pull
> up a loop, YO and draw through 2 loops on
> hook; repeat from ★ 3 times **more**, YO and draw
> through all 5 loops on hook.

AFGHAN BODY

Ch 185 **loosely**, place marker in second ch from
hook for st placement.
Row 1: Working in back ridges of beginning ch
(Fig. 2b, page 137), 2 sc in second ch from hook, sc in
next 5 chs, skip next 2 chs, sc in next 5 chs, 2 sc in
next ch, ★ ch 3, skip next 3 chs, 2 sc in next ch, sc in
next 5 chs, skip next 2 chs, sc in next 5 chs, 2 sc in
next ch; repeat from ★ across: 154 sc and 10 ch-3 sps.
Note: Mark **back** of any stitch on Row 1 as **right**
side.
Row 2 (Right side): Ch 1, turn; working in Back
Loops Only **(Fig. 14, page 140)**, 2 sc in first sc, sc in
next 5 sc, skip next 2 sc, sc in next 5 sc, 2 sc in next
sc, ★ ch 3, 2 sc in next sc, sc in next 5 sc, skip next
2 sc, sc in next 5 sc, 2 sc in next sc; repeat from ★
across.
Repeat Row 2 until Afghan Body measures
approximately 63" from bottom of point, ending by
working a **wrong** side row; do **not** finish off.

EDGING

Rnd 1: Ch 1, turn; working in both loops, (sc, ch 3)
twice in first sc, skip next 2 sc, sc in next sc, ch 3,
skip next sc, sc in next sc, skip next 2 sc, sc in next sc,
[(ch 3, skip next sc, sc in next sc) twice, (ch 3, sc)
twice in next ch-3 sp, (ch 3, skip next sc, sc in next
sc) 3 times, skip next 2 sc, sc in next sc] 10 times,
ch 3, skip next sc, sc in next sc, ch 3, skip next 2 sc,
(sc, ch 3) twice in last sc; skip first row, (sc in end of
next row, ch 3, skip next row) across; working in free
loops **(Fig. 15b, page 140)** and in sps across
beginning ch, sc in marked ch, (ch 3, skip next ch, sc
in next ch) twice, (ch 3, sc) twice in next sp, remove
previous marker and place around last ch-3 made
for st placement, ch 3, [(skip next ch, sc in next ch,
ch 3) twice, sc in next sp, ch 3, skip next 2 chs, sc in
next ch, ch 3, skip next ch, sc in next ch, ch 3, (sc,
ch 3) twice in next sp] across to last 6 chs, (skip next
ch, sc in next ch, ch 3) 3 times; skip first row, (sc in
end of next row, ch 3, skip next row) across; join
with slip st to first sc.
Rnd 2: Do **not** turn; (slip st, ch 5, dc) in first ch-3 sp,
(ch 2, dc in same sp) 3 times, decrease, [(dc, ch 2, dc)
in next ch-3 sp, dc in next ch-3 sp, (ch 2, dc in same
sp) 3 times, (dc, ch 2, dc) in next ch-3 sp, decrease] 10
times, dc in next ch-3 sp, (ch 2, dc in same sp) 4
times, (dc, ch 2, dc) in each ch-3 sp across to marked
ch-3 sp, dc in marked ch-3 sp, (ch 2, dc in same sp) 3
times, remove marker and place around center
ch-2 sp of group just made for st placement, [(dc,
ch 2, dc) in next ch-3 sp, decrease, (dc, ch 2, dc) in
next ch-3 sp, dc in next ch-3 sp, (ch 2, dc in same
sp) 3 times] 10 times, (dc, ch 2, dc) in each ch-3 sp
across; join with slip st to third ch of beginning ch-5.
Rnd 3: (Slip st, ch 1, sc) in first ch-2 sp, ch 5, (sc,
ch 5) twice in next ch-2 sp, [sc in next ch-2 sp, ch 5,
sc in next 2 ch-2 sps, ch 5, sc in next ch-2 sp, ch 5,
(sc, ch 5) twice in next ch-2 sp] 11 times, (sc in next
ch-2 sp, ch 5) across to marked ch-2 sp, (sc, ch 5)
twice in marked ch-2 sp, remove marker, [sc in next
ch-2 sp, ch 5, sc in next 2 ch-2 sps, ch 5, sc in next
ch-2 sp, ch 5, (sc, ch 5) twice in next ch-2 sp] 10
times, (sc in next ch-2 sp, ch 5) across; join with
slip st to first sc.
Rnd 4: Slip st in first ch-5 sp, ch 1, (sc, ch 4, sc in
fourth ch from hook, sc) in same sp and in each
ch-5 sp around; join with slip st to first sc, finish off.

TRANQUILLITY

Richly hued in a deep shade of blue, our luxurious throw will make it easy to relax on an early spring evening. Clusters and spaces come together to create the interesting zigzag pattern.

Finished Size: 50" x 65"

MATERIALS
  Worsted Weight Yarn:
    35 ounces, (990 grams, 2,180 yards)
  Crochet hook, size I (5.50 mm) **or** size needed
    for gauge

GAUGE: In pattern, one repeat = 4"; 7 rows = 4^1/$_4$ "

Gauge Swatch: 8^1/$_4$ "w x 4^1/$_4$ "h
Ch 26 **loosely**.
Work same as Afghan Body for 7 rows.
Finish off.

Note: Each row is worked across length of Afghan.

STITCH GUIDE

> **CLUSTER**
> Ch 3, YO, insert hook in third ch from hook, YO
> and pull up a loop, YO and draw through
> 2 loops on hook, YO, insert hook in same ch, YO
> and pull up a loop, YO and draw through
> 2 loops on hook, YO and draw through all
> 3 loops on hook (*Figs. 11a & b, page 139*).

AFGHAN BODY

Ch 194 **loosely**.
Row 1: Sc in second ch from hook, ★ (work Cluster, skip next 2 chs, sc in next ch) twice, (ch 5, skip next 2 chs, sc in next ch) twice; repeat from ★ across: 32 Clusters and 32 ch-5 sps.
Row 2 (Right side): Ch 5 **(counts as first tr plus ch 1, now and throughout)**, turn; sc in next ch-5 sp, ch 5, sc in next ch-5 sp, (work Cluster, sc in ch-2 sp of next Cluster) twice, ★ (ch 5, sc in next ch-5 sp) twice, (work Cluster, sc in ch-2 sp of next Cluster) twice; repeat from ★ across to last sc, ch 1, tr in last sc.
Note: Mark Row 2 as **right** side.
Row 3: Ch 1, turn; sc in first tr, ch 5, skip next ch-1 sp, (sc in ch-2 sp of next Cluster, work Cluster) twice, ★ (sc in next ch-5 sp, ch 5) twice, (sc in ch-2 sp of next Cluster, work Cluster) twice; repeat from ★

across to last 2 sps, sc in next ch-5 sp, ch 5, skip next ch-1 sp, sc in last tr.
Row 4: Ch 5, turn; sc in next ch-5 sp, (work Cluster, sc in ch-2 sp of next Cluster) twice, ★ (ch 5, sc in next ch-5 sp) twice, (work Cluster, sc in ch-2 sp of next Cluster) twice; repeat from ★ across to last ch-5 sp, ch 5, sc in last ch-5 sp, ch 1, tr in last sc.
Row 5: Ch 1, turn; sc in first tr, ch 5, skip next ch-1 sp, sc in next ch-5 sp, ch 5, (sc in ch-2 sp of next Cluster, work Cluster) twice, ★ (sc in next ch-5 sp, ch 5) twice, (sc in ch-2 sp of next Cluster, work Cluster) twice; repeat from ★ across to last ch-1 sp, skip last ch-1 sp, sc in last tr.
Row 6: Ch 5, turn; (sc in ch-2 sp of next Cluster, work Cluster) twice, ★ (sc in next ch-5 sp, ch 5) twice, (sc in ch-2 sp of next Cluster, work Cluster) twice; repeat from ★ across to last 2 ch-5 sps, sc in next ch-5 sp, ch 5, sc in next ch-5 sp, ch 1, tr in last sc.
Row 7: Ch 1, turn; sc in first tr, ch 5, skip next ch-1 sp, sc in next ch-5 sp, (work Cluster, sc in ch-2 sp of next Cluster) twice, ★ (ch 5, sc in next ch-5 sp) twice, (work Cluster, sc in ch-2 sp of next Cluster) twice; repeat from ★ across to last ch-1 sp, ch 5, skip last ch-1 sp, sc in last tr.
Row 8: Ch 5, turn; sc in next ch-5 sp, ch 5, (sc in ch-2 sp of next Cluster, work Cluster) twice, ★ (sc in next ch-5 sp, ch 5) twice, (sc in ch-2 sp of next Cluster, work Cluster) twice; repeat from ★ across to last ch-5 sp, sc in last ch-5 sp, ch 1, tr in last sc.
Row 9: Ch 1, turn; sc in first tr, (work Cluster, sc in ch-2 sp of next Cluster) twice, ★ (ch 5, sc in next ch-5 sp) twice, (work Cluster, sc in ch-2 sp of next Cluster) twice; repeat from ★ across to last 2 sps, ch 5, sc in next ch-5 sp, ch 5, sc in last tr.
Row 10: Ch 5, turn; sc in next ch-5 sp, ch 5, sc in next ch-5 sp, (work Cluster, sc in ch-2 sp of next Cluster) twice, ★ (ch 5, sc in next ch-5 sp) twice, (work Cluster, sc in ch-2 sp of next Cluster) twice; repeat from ★ across to last sc, ch 1, tr in last sc.
Repeat Rows 3-10 until Afghan Body measures approximately 49" from beginning ch, ending by working Row 9; do **not** finish off.

Continued on page 12.

Next Row: Ch 5, turn; sc in next ch-5 sp, ch 2, sc in next ch-5 sp, (ch 2, sc in ch-2 sp of next Cluster) twice, ★ (ch 2, sc in next ch-5 sp) twice, (ch 2, sc in ch-2 sp of next Cluster) twice; repeat from ★ across to last sc, ch 1, tr in last sc; do **not** finish off: 66 sts and 65 sps.

EDGING
FIRST SIDE
Row 1: Ch 1, turn; sc in first tr, ★ ch 1, skip next ch, sc in next sc, ch 1, skip next ch, sc in next ch, ch 1, skip next sc, sc in next ch; repeat from ★ across to last tr, sc in last tr: 98 sc and 96 ch-1 sps.

Row 2: Ch 1, turn; slip st in first sc, ch 2, skip next sc, (slip st in next ch-1 sp, ch 2) across to last ch-1 sp, slip st in last ch-1 sp and in last sc; finish off.

SECOND SIDE
Row 1: With **wrong** side facing and working in free loops of beginning ch *(Fig. 15b, page 140)*, join yarn with sc in first ch *(see Joining With Sc, page 140)*; (ch 1, skip next ch, sc in next ch) across: 97 sc and 96 ch-1 sps.

Row 2: Ch 1, turn; slip st in first sc and in next ch-1 sp, ch 2, (slip st in next ch-1 sp, ch 2) across to last ch-1 sp, slip st in last ch-1 sp and in last sc; finish off.

GLORIOUS LILACS

Inspired by spring's glorious lilacs, this plush wrap is a wonderful way to welcome the most invigorating season of the year. The easy project is worked with a jumbo Q hook using three strands of worsted weight yarn.

Finished Size: 45" x 62¹/₂"

MATERIALS
Worsted Weight Yarn:
   Lilac - 43 ounces, (1,220 grams, 2,800 yards)
   Ecru - 31 ounces, (880 grams, 2,020 yards)
   Green - 6 ounces, (170 grams, 390 yards)
Crochet hook, size Q (15.00 mm)
Yarn needle

Afghan is worked holding three strands of yarn together.

GAUGE: Each Square = 5¹/₂"; Each Strip = 7¹/₂"

Gauge Swatch: 4" square
Work same as Square through Rnd 2.

STRIP (Make 6)
SQUARE (Make 11)
Rnd 1 (Right side): With Green, ch 2, 8 sc in second ch from hook; join with slip st to first sc, finish off. *Note:* Mark Rnd 1 as **right** side.

Rnd 2: With **right** side facing, join Lilac with sc in any sc *(see Joining With Sc, page 140)*; tr in same st, (sc, tr) in next sc and in each sc around pushing tr to **right** side; join with slip st to first sc, finish off: 16 sts.

Rnd 3: With **right** side facing, join Ecru with sc in any sc; 2 sc in same st, skip next tr, (2 dc, ch 2, 2 dc) in next sc, skip next tr, ★ 3 sc in next sc, skip next tr, (2 dc, ch 2, 2 dc) in next sc, skip next tr; repeat from ★ 2 times **more**; join with slip st to first sc, finish off: 28 sts and 4 ch-2 sps.

STRIP ASSEMBLY
With Ecru and working through **inside** loops only, whipstitch Squares together *(Fig. 20, page 142)*, beginning in second ch of first corner ch-2 and ending in first ch of next corner ch-2.

EDGING
With **right** side facing, join Lilac with slip st in any corner ch-2 sp; ch 3, (dc, ch 2, 2 dc) in same sp, dc in each st around working dc in each joining and (2 dc, ch 2, 2 dc) in each corner ch-2 sp; join with slip st to top of beginning ch-3, finish off.

AFGHAN ASSEMBLY
With Lilac and working through **inside** loops only, whipstitch Strips together beginning in second ch of first corner ch-2 and ending in first ch of next corner ch-2.

SOUTHERN BLOSSOMS

*This elegant throw is as beautiful as it is cozy! Picot stitches create a lacy edging,
as three-dimensional petals give a realistic appearance to the magnolia blossoms.*

Finished Size: 50" x 64"

MATERIALS
Worsted Weight Yarn:
Pink - 37 ounces, (1,050 grams, 2,430 yards)
White - 10 ounces, (280 grams, 655 yards)
Green - 6^1/$_2$ ounces, (180 grams, 425 yards)
Crochet hook, size H (5.00 mm) **or** size needed
for gauge
Yarn needle

GAUGE: Each Square = 6^3/$_4$ "

STITCH GUIDE

> **PICOT**
> Ch 4, slip st in fourth ch from hook.
> **V-ST**
> (Dc, ch 1, dc) in sp indicated.

SQUARE (Make 63)
With White, ch 5; join with slip st to form a ring.
Rnd 1 (Right side): Ch 1, (sc in ring, ch 4) 8 times;
join with slip st to first sc: 8 ch-4 sps.
Note: Mark Rnd 1 as **right** side.
Rnd 2: Slip st in first ch-4 sp, ch 1, (sc, dc, 2 tr, dc,
sc) in same sp **(Petal made)**, ch 1, ★ (sc, dc, 2 tr, dc,
sc) in next ch-4 sp, ch 1; repeat from ★ around; join
with slip st to first sc: 8 Petals.
Rnd 3: Turn; slip st in first ch-1 sp, ch 3, working in
front of Petals, (slip st in next ch-1 sp, ch 3) around;
join with slip st to first slip st, finish off: 8 ch-3 sps.
Rnd 4: With **right** side facing, join Green with slip st
in any ch-3 sp; ch 3 **(counts as first dc, now and
throughout)**, 3 dc in same sp, 4 dc in next ch-3 sp,
ch 3, (4 dc in each of next 2 ch-3 sps, ch 3) around;
join with slip st to first dc, finish off: 32 dc and
4 ch-3 sps.
Rnd 5: With **right** side facing, join Pink with slip st
in any ch-3 sp; ch 3, (dc, ch 3, 2 dc) in same sp, dc in
each dc across to next ch-3 sp, ★ (2 dc, ch 3, 2 dc) in
ch-3 sp, dc in each dc across to next ch-3 sp; repeat
from ★ around; join with slip st to first dc: 48 dc and
4 ch-3 sps.

Rnd 6: Slip st in next dc and in next ch-3 sp, ch 7
(counts as first dc plus ch 4, now and throughout),
slip st in fourth ch from hook, (dc, ch 3, dc, work
Picot, dc) in same sp, (ch 2, skip next 2 dc, dc in next
dc, work Picot, skip next dc, dc in next dc) twice,
★ ch 2, in next ch-3 sp work (dc, Picot, dc, ch 3, dc,
Picot, dc), (ch 2, skip next 2 dc, dc in next dc, work
Picot, skip next dc, dc in next dc) twice; repeat from
★ around, ch 1, sc in first dc to form last ch-2 sp:
12 ch-2 sps and 4 ch-3 sps.
Rnd 7: Ch 4 **(counts as first dc plus ch 1)**, dc in
same sp (beginning V-St made), ch 2, work (V-St,
ch 3, V-St) in next ch-3 sp, ch 2, ★ (work V-St in next
ch-2 sp, ch 2) 3 times, work (V-St, ch 3, V-St) in next
ch-3 sp, ch 2; repeat from ★ 2 times **more**, (work V-St
in next ch-2 sp, ch 2) twice; join with slip st to first
dc: 40 sps.
Rnd 8: Slip st in first ch-1 sp, ch 3, dc in same sp,
★ 2 dc in each sp across to next corner ch-3 sp, (3 dc,
ch 1, 3 dc) in corner ch-3 sp; repeat from ★ 3 times
more, 2 dc in each sp across; join with slip st to first
dc, finish off: 96 dc and 4 ch-1 sps.

ASSEMBLY
With Pink and working through **inside** loops only,
whipstitch Squares together forming 7 vertical strips
of 9 Squares each *(Fig. 20, page 142)*, beginning in
first corner ch and ending in next corner ch; then
whipstitch strips together in same manner.

EDGING
Rnd 1: With **right** side of short end facing, join
Green with sc in top right corner ch-1 sp *(see Joining
With Sc, page 140)*; 2 sc in same sp, † work
181 sc evenly spaced across to next corner ch-1 sp,
3 sc in corner ch-1 sp, work 233 sc evenly spaced
across to next corner ch-1 sp †, 3 sc in corner ch-1 sp,
repeat from † to † once; join with slip st to first sc,
finish off: 840 sc.

Rnd 2: With **right** side facing, join Pink with slip st in first sc of any corner 3-sc group; ch 7, slip st in fourth ch from hook, dc in same st at base of ch-7, ★ ch 2, skip next sc, (dc, work Picot, dc) in next sc; repeat from ★ around to last sc, ch 1, skip last sc, sc in first dc to form last ch-2 sp.

Rnd 3: Ch 7, slip st in fourth ch from hook, dc in same sp, ch 2, ★ (dc, work Picot, dc) in next ch-2 sp, ch 2; repeat from ★ around; join with slip st to first dc, finish off.

AROUND THE BLOCK

Somewhere over the rainbow is a special friend who will love this gorgeous wrap!
Its petite blocks strengthen in color as they radiate out from the center.

Finished Size: 45" x 57"

MATERIALS
Worsted Weight Yarn:
    White - 8 ounces, (230 grams, 525 yards)
    Yellow - 2 ounces, (60 grams, 135 yards)
    Peach - 3 ounces, (90 grams, 200 yards)
    Pink - 4 ounces, (110 grams, 265 yards)
    Green - 5 ounces, (140 grams, 330 yards)
    Blue - 6 ounces, (170 grams, 395 yards)
    Lt Purple - 8 ounces, (230 grams, 525 yards)
    Purple - 8 ounces, (230 grams, 525 yards)
Crochet hook, size H (5.00 mm) **or** size needed
    for gauge

GAUGE: Each Square = 3"

STITCH GUIDE

BEGINNING CLUSTER
Ch 2, ★ YO, insert hook in sp indicated, YO and
pull up a loop, YO and draw through 2 loops on
hook; repeat from ★ once **more**, YO and draw
through all 3 loops on hook *(Figs. 11a & b,
page 139)*.
CLUSTER
★ YO, insert hook in sp indicated, YO and pull
up a loop, YO and draw through 2 loops on
hook; repeat from ★ 2 times **more**, YO and draw
through all 4 loops on hook *(Figs. 11a & b,
page 139)*.
PICOT
Ch 1, sc in back ridge of ch just made *(Fig. 2b,
page 137)*, ch 1.

SQUARE

Make the following number of Squares in the
color indicated: Yellow - 21; Peach - 24; Pink - 32;
Green - 40; Blue - 48; Lt Purple - 56; Purple - 64.

Ch 5, join with slip st to form a ring.
Rnd 1 (Right side): Work (Beginning Cluster, ch 3,
Cluster) in ring, ch 1, ★ work (Cluster, ch 3, Cluster)
in ring, ch 1; repeat from ★ 2 times **more**; join with
slip st to Beginning Cluster: 8 Clusters.
Note: Mark Rnd 1 as **right** side.

Rnd 2: Slip st in first ch-3 sp, work (Beginning
Cluster, ch 3, Cluster) in same sp, ch 1, (dc, ch 1)
twice in next ch-1 sp, ★ work (Cluster, ch 3, Cluster)
in next ch-3 sp, ch 1, (dc, ch 1) twice in next ch-1 sp;
repeat from ★ around; join with slip st to Beginning
Cluster, finish off.

JOINING
Note: Because there is no stability in the lace joining,
the Squares may appear to jog to the right or left
when your Afghan is complete. This is characteristic
of the design and cannot be avoided.

Using Placement Diagram as a guide, page 18, join
Squares into 15 vertical strips of 19 Squares each as
follows; then join strips in same manner.

Holding Squares side by side, with **right** sides
facing, and working in Back Loops Only *(Fig. 14,
page 140)*, join White with slip st in center ch of any
corner ch-3 of **first Square**; ch 1, slip st in center ch
of any corner ch-3 of **second Square**, ch 1, ★ skip
next ch of **first Square**, slip st in next st, ch 1, skip
next ch of **second Square**, slip st in next st, ch 1;
repeat from ★ across to next corner ch-3, skip next
ch of **first Square**, slip st in center ch of corner ch-3,
ch 1, skip next ch of **second Square**, slip st in center
ch of corner ch-3; finish off.

EDGING
With **right** side facing and working in Back Loops
Only, join White with slip st in center ch of any
corner ch-3 of Afghan; work Picot, skip next st,
(slip st in next st, work Picot, skip next st) around;
join with slip st to first st, finish off.

PLACEMENT DIAGRAM

G	G	G	G	G	G	G	G	G	G	G	G	G
G	F	F	F	F	F	F	F	F	F	F	F	G
G	F	E	E	E	E	E	E	E	E	E	F	G
G	F	E	D	D	D	D	D	D	D	E	F	G
G	F	E	D	C	C	C	C	C	C	D	E	F	G
G	F	E	D	C	B	B	B	B	C	D	E	F	G
G	F	E	D	C	B	A	A	A	B	C	D	E	F	G
G	F	E	D	C	B	A	A	A	B	C	D	E	F	G
G	F	E	D	C	B	A	A	A	B	C	D	E	F	G
G	F	E	D	C	B	A	A	A	B	C	D	E	F	G
G	F	E	D	C	B	A	A	A	B	C	D	E	F	G
G	F	E	D	C	B	A	A	A	B	C	D	E	F	G
G	F	E	D	C	B	A	A	A	B	C	D	E	F	G
G	F	E	D	C	B	B	B	B	C	D	E	F	G
G	F	E	D	C	C	C	C	C	C	D	E	F	G
G	F	E	D	D	D	D	D	D	D	E	F	G
G	F	E	E	E	E	E	E	E	E	E	F	G
G	F	F	F	F	F	F	F	F	F	F	F	G
G	G	G	G	G	G	G	G	G	G	G	G	G

KEY

A - Yellow

B - Peach

C - Pink

D - Green

E - Blue

F - Lt Purple

G - Purple

GARDEN OF FLOWERS

Light and airy, this throw is the picture of perfection. Lacy squares with swirling blooms come together to create a gardenful of grace.

Finished Size: 53" x 70"

MATERIALS

Worsted Weight Yarn:
Yellow - $3^{1}/_{2}$ ounces, (100 grams, 230 yards)
Rose - 14 ounces, (400 grams, 920 yards)
Ecru - $13^{1}/_{2}$ ounces, (380 grams, 885 yards)
Green - 8 ounces, (230 grams, 525 yards)
Crochet hook, size I (5.50 mm) **or** size needed for gauge

GAUGE: One Square = $8^{1}/_{2}$"

STITCH GUIDE

DOUBLE BOBBLE
Ch 3, dc in third ch from hook, ch 4, dc in third ch from hook.

FIRST SQUARE

Rnd 1 (Right side): With Yellow, ch 2, 8 sc in second ch from hook; join with slip st to first sc: 8 sc.
Note: Mark Rnd 1 as **right** side.
Rnd 2: Work Double Bobble, ★ slip st in next sc, work Double Bobble; repeat from ★ around; join with slip st at base of first Double Bobble, finish off: 8 Double Bobbles.
Rnd 3: With **right** side facing, join Rose with sc in center of any Double Bobble *(see Joining With Sc, page 140)*; ch 3, sc in same sp, ch 3, (sc, ch 3) twice in center of next Double Bobble and in center of each Double Bobble around; join with slip st to first sc: 16 ch-3 sps.
Rnd 4: Slip st in first ch-3 sp, ch 3 **(counts as first dc)**, 4 dc in same sp, ch 1, sc in next ch-3 sp, ch 1, ★ 5 dc in next ch-3 sp, ch 1, sc in next ch-3 sp, ch 1; repeat from ★ around; join with slip st to first dc, finish off: 40 dc.
Rnd 5: With **right** side facing, join Ecru with slip st in any sc; ch 6, dc in same st, ch 3, skip next 2 dc, sc in next dc, ch 3, ★ (dc, ch 3) twice in next sc, skip next 2 dc, sc in next dc, ch 3; repeat from ★ around; join with slip st to third ch of beginning ch-6: 24 ch-3 sps.

Rnd 6: Slip st in next ch-3 sp, ch 4, 6 tr in same sp, dc in next ch-3 sp, ch 3, (sc in next ch-3 sp, ch 3) 3 times, dc in next ch-3 sp, ★ 7 tr in next ch-3 sp, dc in next ch-3 sp, ch 3, (sc in next ch-3 sp, ch 3) 3 times, dc in next ch-3 sp; repeat from ★ around; join with slip st to top of beginning ch-4: 16 ch-3 sps.
Rnd 7: Slip st in next tr, ch 4, ★ † skip next tr, (dc, ch 2, tr, ch 2, dc) in next tr (corner made), ch 2, skip next tr, hdc in next tr, ch 2, (hdc in next ch-3 sp, ch 2) 4 times †, skip next dc and next tr, hdc in next tr, ch 2; repeat from ★ 2 times **more**, then repeat from † to † once; join with slip st to second ch of beginning ch-4, finish off: 36 ch-2 sps.
Rnd 8: With **right** side facing, join Rose with slip st in first ch-2 sp after any corner tr; ch 4, dc in same sp, (dc, ch 1, dc) in each of next 8 ch-2 sps, ch 3 (corner made), ★ (dc, ch 1, dc) in each of next 9 ch-2 sps, ch 3 (corner made); repeat from ★ around; join with slip st to third ch of beginning ch-4, finish off: 36 ch-1 sps.
Rnd 9: With **right** side facing, join Green with sc in any corner ch-3 sp; ch 5, sc in same sp, ch 3, (sc in next ch-1 sp, ch 3) 9 times, ★ (sc, ch 5, sc) in next corner ch-3 sp, ch 3, (sc in next ch-1 sp, ch 3) 9 times; repeat from ★ around; join with slip st to first sc, finish off.

Continued on page 20.

ADDITIONAL SQUARES

(Make 47)

Rnds 1-8: Work same as First Square: 36 ch-1 sps.

Rnd 9 (Joining rnd)**:** Referring to Placement Diagram, work One or Two Side Joining (*Fig. 19, page 141*), as follows:

ONE SIDE JOINING

With **right** side facing, join Green with sc in any corner ch-3 sp, ch 2; holding Squares with **right** sides facing, slip st in third ch of corner ch-5 on **adjacent Square** (first corner joined), ch 2, sc in same corner as joining on **new Square**, ch 1, slip st in second ch of next ch-3 on **adjacent Square**, ch 1, (sc in next ch-1 sp on **new Square**, ch 1, slip st in second ch of next ch-3 on **adjacent Square**, ch 1) across to next corner ch-3 sp, sc in corner **on new Square**, ch 2, slip st in third ch of corner ch-5 on **adjacent Square**, ch 2, sc in same corner on **new Square** (second corner joined), ch 3; working around remaining sides of **new Square**, (sc in next ch-1 sp, ch 3) 9 times, ★ (sc, ch 5, sc) in next ch-3 sp, ch 3, (sc in next ch-1 sp, ch 3) 9 times; repeat from ★ around; join with slip st to first sc, finish off.

TWO SIDE JOINING

With **right** side facing, join Green with sc in any corner ch-3 sp, ch 2; holding Square and Afghan with **right** sides facing, slip st in third ch of corner ch-5 on **adjacent Square** (first corner joined), ch 2, sc in same corner as joining on **new Square**, † ch 1, slip st in second ch of next ch-3 on **adjacent Square**, ch 1, (sc in next ch-1 sp on **new Square**, ch 1, slip st in second ch of next ch-3 on **adjacent Square**, ch 1) across to next corner ch-3 sp, sc in corner on **new Square**, ch 2, slip st in same ch as previous joining on **adjacent Squares**, ch 2, sc in same corner on **new Square** † (second corner joined), repeat from † to † once (third corner joined), ch 3; working around remaining sides of **new Square**, (sc in next ch-1 sp, ch 3) 9 times, (sc, ch 5, sc) in next ch-3 sp, ch 3, (sc in next ch-1 sp, ch 3) 9 times; join with slip st to first sc, finish off.

PLACEMENT DIAGRAM

A	1	1	1	1	1
1	2	2	2	2	2
1	2	2	2	2	2
1	2	2	2	2	2
1	2	2	2	2	2
1	2	2	2	2	2
1	2	2	2	2	2
1	2	2	2	2	2

KEY

A	- First Square
1	- One Side Joining
2	- Two Side Joining

EDGING

Rnd 1: With **right** side facing, join Green with sc in any corner ch-5 sp; ch 3, sc in same sp, ch 3, ★ † (sc in next ch-3 sp, ch 3) 10 times, [sc in same ch as previous joining, ch 3, (sc in next ch-3 sp, ch 3) 10 times] across to next corner ch-5 sp †, (sc, ch 3) twice in corner; repeat from ★ 2 times **more**, then repeat from † to † once; join with slip st to first sc.

Rnd 2: Slip st in corner ch-3 sp, ch 1, (sc, ch 2) twice in same corner, ★ † (sc in next ch-3 sp, ch 2) across to next corner ch-3 sp †, (sc, ch 2) twice in corner; repeat from ★ 2 times **more**, then repeat from † to † once; join with slip st to first sc.

Rnd 3: Ch 3, dc in same sc, (slip st, ch 3, dc) in next sc and in each sc around; join with slip st at base of beginning ch-3, finish off.

BUNNY LOVE

Precious bunnies and sweet hearts abound on a field of filet crochet in this springtime coverlet. It's sure to warm the heart of someone dear to you.

Finished Size: 66¹/₂ " x 83"

MATERIALS
Worsted Weight Yarn:
60 ounces, (1,700 grams, 3,390 yards)
Crochet hook, size I (5.50 mm) **or** size needed for gauge

GAUGE: In pattern, 12 dc = 4"; 7 rows = 4¹/₂ "

Gauge Swatch: 4"w x 4¹/₂ "h
Ch 14 **loosely**.
Row 1: Dc in fourth ch from hook **(3 skipped chs count as first dc)** and in each ch across: 12 dc.
Rows 2-7: Ch 3 **(counts as first dc)**, turn; dc in next dc and in each dc across.
Finish off.

AFGHAN
Ch 201 **loosely**.
Row 1 (Right side): Dc in back ridge of fourth ch from hook *(Fig. 2b, page 137)* and in each ch across **(3 skipped chs count as first dc)**: 199 dc.
Row 2: Ch 3 **(counts as first dc, now and throughout)**, turn; dc in next dc and in each dc across.
Row 3: Ch 3, turn; dc in next 4 dc, ch 1, (skip next dc, dc in next dc, ch 1) 10 times, ★ skip next dc, dc in next 3 dc, ch 1, (skip next dc, dc in next dc, ch 1) 10 times; repeat from ★ across to last 6 dc, skip next dc, dc in last 5 dc: 111 dc and 88 ch-1 sps.
Row 4: Ch 3, turn; dc in next 4 dc, ★ † ch 1, (dc in next dc, ch 1) 4 times, dc in next dc and in next ch-1 sp, (dc in next dc, ch 1) 5 times †, dc in next 3 dc; repeat from ★ 6 times **more**, then repeat from † to † once, dc in last 5 dc: 119 dc and 80 ch-1 sps.
Row 5: Ch 3, turn; dc in next 4 dc, ★ † (ch 1, dc in next dc) 4 times, dc in next ch-1 sp, dc in next 3 dc and in next ch-1 sp, (dc in next dc, ch 1) 4 times †, dc in next 3 dc; repeat from ★ 6 times **more**, then repeat from † to † once, dc in last 5 dc: 135 dc and 64 ch-1 sps.

Row 6: Ch 3, turn; dc in next 4 dc, ★ † (ch 1, dc in next dc) 3 times, dc in next ch-1 sp, dc in next 7 dc and in next ch-1 sp, (dc in next dc, ch 1) 3 times †, dc in next 3 dc; repeat from ★ 6 times **more**, then repeat from † to † once, dc in last 5 dc: 151 dc and 48 ch-1 sps.
Row 7: Ch 3, turn; dc in next 4 dc, ★ † (ch 1, dc in next dc) twice, dc in next ch-1 sp, dc in next 11 dc and in next ch-1 sp, (dc in next dc, ch 1) twice †, dc in next 3 dc; repeat from ★ 6 times **more**, then repeat from † to † once, dc in last 5 dc: 167 dc and 32 ch-1 sps.
Row 8: Ch 3, turn; dc in next 4 dc, ★ † ch 1, dc in next dc, dc in next ch-1 sp and in next 15 dc, dc in next ch-1 sp and in next dc, ch 1 †, dc in next 3 dc; repeat from ★ 6 times **more**, then repeat from † to † once, dc in last 5 dc: 183 dc and 16 ch-1 sps.
Rows 9 and 10: Ch 3, turn; dc in next 4 dc, ch 1, dc in next 19 dc, ch 1, ★ dc in next 3 dc, ch 1, dc in next 19 dc, ch 1; repeat from ★ across to last 5 dc, dc in last 5 dc.
Row 11: Ch 3, turn; dc in next 4 dc, ch 1, dc in next 9 dc, ch 1, skip next dc, dc in next 9 dc, ch 1, ★ dc in next 3 dc, ch 1, dc in next 9 dc, ch 1, skip next dc, dc in next 9 dc, ch 1; repeat from ★ across to last 5 dc, dc in last 5 dc: 175 dc and 24 ch-1 sps.
Row 12: Ch 3, turn; dc in next 4 dc, ★ † ch 1, dc in next dc, ch 1, skip next dc, dc in next 5 dc, ch 1, skip next dc, (dc in next dc, ch 1) twice, skip next dc, dc in next 5 dc, ch 1, skip next dc, dc in next dc, ch 1 †, dc in next 3 dc; repeat from ★ 6 times **more**, then repeat from † to † once, dc in last 5 dc: 143 dc and 56 ch-1 sps.
Row 13: Ch 3, turn; dc in next 4 dc, ★ † ch 1, (dc in next dc, ch 1) twice, (skip next dc, dc in next dc, ch 1) twice, (dc in next dc, ch 1) 3 times, (skip next dc, dc in next dc, ch 1) twice, dc in next dc, ch 1 †, dc in next 3 dc; repeat from ★ 6 times **more**, then repeat from † to † once, dc in last 5 dc: 111 dc and 88 ch-1 sps.
Row 14: Ch 3, turn; dc in next dc and in each dc and each ch-1 sp across; do **not** finish off: 199 dc.

Continued on page 24.

Row 15: Ch 3, turn; dc in next 4 dc, ch 1, (skip next dc, dc in next dc, ch 1) 22 times, ★ skip next dc, dc in next 3 dc, ch 1, (skip next dc, dc in next dc, ch 1) 22 times; repeat from ★ 2 times **more**, skip next dc, dc in last 5 dc: 107 dc and 92 ch-1 sps.

Row 16: Ch 3, turn; dc in next 4 dc, † (ch 1, dc in next dc) 3 times, (dc in next ch-1 sp and in next dc) 18 times, ch 1, dc in next dc, ch 1, dc in next 3 dc, (ch 1, dc in next dc) twice, (dc in next ch-1 sp and in next dc) 18 times, ch 1, (dc in next dc, ch 1) twice †, dc in next 3 dc, repeat from † to † once, dc in last 5 dc: 179 dc and 20 ch-1 sps.

Row 17: Ch 3, turn; dc in next 4 dc, † ch 1, (dc in next dc, ch 1) twice, dc in next 37 dc, ch 1, dc in next dc, ch 1, dc in next 3 dc, ch 1, dc in next dc, ch 1, dc in next 37 dc, ch 1, (dc in next dc, ch 1) twice †, dc in next 3 dc, repeat from † to † once, dc in last 5 dc.

Row 18: Ch 3, turn; dc in next 4 dc, † ch 1, (dc in next dc and in next ch-1 sp) twice, dc in next 37 dc, ch 1, dc in next dc, ch 1, dc in next 3 dc, ch 1, dc in next dc, ch 1, dc in next 37 dc, (dc in next ch-1 sp and in next dc) twice, ch 1 †, dc in next 3 dc, repeat from † to † once, dc in last 5 dc: 187 dc and 12 ch-1 sps.

Row 19: Ch 3, turn; dc in next 4 dc, † ch 1, dc in next 39 dc, ch 1, skip next dc, (dc in next dc, ch 1) twice, dc in next 3 dc, ch 1, (dc in next dc, ch 1) twice, skip next dc, dc in next 39 dc, ch 1 †, dc in next 3 dc, repeat from † to † once, dc in last 5 dc: 183 dc and 16 ch-1 sps.

Row 20: Ch 3, turn; dc in next 4 dc, † ch 1, dc in next 37 dc, ch 1, skip next dc, (dc in next dc, ch 1) 3 times, dc in next 3 dc, ch 1, (dc in next dc, ch 1) 3 times, skip next dc, dc in next 37 dc, ch 1 †, dc in next 3 dc, repeat from † to † once, dc in last 5 dc: 179 dc and 20 ch-1 sps.

Row 21: Ch 3, turn; dc in next 4 dc, † ch 1, dc in next dc, ch 1, skip next dc, dc in next 33 dc, ch 1, skip next dc, (dc in next dc, ch 1) 4 times, dc in next 3 dc, ch 1, (dc in next dc, ch 1) 4 times, skip next dc, dc in next 33 dc, ch 1, skip next dc, dc in next dc, ch 1 †, dc in next 3 dc, repeat from † to † once, dc in last 5 dc: 171 dc and 28 ch-1 sps.

Row 22: Ch 3, turn; dc in next 4 dc, † ch 1, (dc in next dc, ch 1) twice, skip next dc, dc in next 29 dc, ch 1, skip next dc, (dc in next dc, ch 1) 5 times, dc in next 3 dc, ch 1, (dc in next dc, ch 1) 5 times, skip next dc, dc in next 29 dc, ch 1, skip next dc, (dc in next dc, ch 1) twice †, dc in next 3 dc, repeat from † to † once, dc in last 5 dc: 163 dc and 36 ch-1 sps.

Row 23: Ch 3, turn; dc in next 4 dc, † ch 1, (dc in next dc, ch 1) twice, dc in next 29 dc and in next ch-1 sp, (dc in next dc, ch 1) 5 times, dc in next 3 dc, (ch 1, dc in next dc) 5 times, dc in next ch-1 sp and in next 29 dc, ch 1, (dc in next dc, ch 1) twice †, dc in next 3 dc, repeat from † to † once, dc in last 5 dc: 167 dc and 32 ch-1 sps.

Row 24: Ch 3, turn; dc in next 4 dc, † ch 1, (dc in next dc, ch 1) 3 times, skip next dc, dc in next 29 dc, (dc in next ch-1 sp and in next dc) 3 times, ch 1, dc in next dc, ch 1, dc in next 3 dc, ch 1, dc in next dc, ch 1, (dc in next dc and in next ch-1 sp) 3 times, dc in next 29 dc, ch 1, skip next dc, (dc in next dc, ch 1) 3 times †, dc in next 3 dc, repeat from † to † once, dc in last 5 dc: 175 dc and 24 ch-1 sps.

Row 25: Ch 3, turn; dc in next 4 dc, † ch 1, (dc in next dc, ch 1) 3 times, dc in next 35 dc, dc in next ch-1 sp and in next dc, ch 1, dc in next 3 dc, ch 1, dc in next dc, dc in next ch-1 sp and in next 35 dc, ch 1, (dc in next dc, ch 1) 3 times †, dc in next 3 dc, repeat from † to † once, dc in last 5 dc: 179 dc and 20 ch-1 sps.

Row 26: Ch 3, turn; dc in next 4 dc, † ch 1, (dc in next dc, ch 1) 4 times, skip next dc, dc in next 35 dc, ch 1, dc in next 3 dc, ch 1, dc in next 35 dc, ch 1, skip next dc, (dc in next dc, ch 1) 4 times †, dc in next 3 dc, repeat from † to † once, dc in last 5 dc: 175 dc and 24 ch-1 sps.

Row 27: Ch 3, turn; dc in next 4 dc, † ch 1, (dc in next dc, ch 1) 5 times, skip next dc, dc in next 33 dc, ch 1, dc in next 3 dc, ch 1, dc in next 33 dc, ch 1, skip next dc, (dc in next dc, ch 1) 5 times †, dc in next 3 dc, repeat from † to † once, dc in last 5 dc: 171 dc and 28 ch-1 sps.

Row 28: Ch 3, turn; dc in next 4 dc, † ch 1, (dc in next dc, ch 1) 6 times, skip next dc, dc in next 25 dc, ch 1, skip next dc, dc in next 5 dc, ch 1, dc in next 3 dc, ch 1, dc in next 5 dc, ch 1, skip next dc, dc in next 25 dc, ch 1, skip next dc, (dc in next dc, ch 1) 6 times †, dc in next 3 dc, repeat from † to † once, dc in last 5 dc: 163 dc and 36 ch-1 sps.

Row 29: Ch 3, turn; dc in next 4 dc, † ch 1, (dc in next dc, ch 1) 7 times, skip next dc, (dc in next dc, ch 1, skip next dc) 6 times, dc in next 11 dc, dc in next ch-1 sp and in next 5 dc, ch 1, dc in next 3 dc, ch 1, dc in next 5 dc, dc in next ch-1 sp and in next 11 dc, ch 1, (skip next dc, dc in next dc, ch 1) 7 times, (dc in next dc, ch 1) 6 times †, dc in next 3 dc, repeat from † to † once, dc in last 5 dc: 139 dc and 60 ch-1 sps.

Row 30: Ch 3, turn; dc in next 4 dc, † ch 1, (dc in next dc, ch 1) 13 times, dc in next 17 dc, ch 1, dc in next 3 dc, ch 1, dc in next 17 dc, ch 1, (dc in next dc, ch 1) 13 times †, dc in next 3 dc, repeat from † to † once, dc in last 5 dc.

Row 31: Ch 3, turn; dc in next 4 dc, † (ch 1, dc in next dc) 13 times, dc in next ch-1 sp and in next 15 dc, ch 1, skip next dc, dc in next dc, ch 1, dc in next 3 dc, ch 1, dc in next dc, ch 1, skip next dc, dc in next 15 dc and in next ch-1 sp, (dc in next dc, ch 1) 13 times †, dc in next 3 dc, repeat from † to † once, dc in last 5 dc.

Row 32: Ch 3, turn; dc in next 4 dc, † (ch 1, dc in next dc) 4 times, dc in next ch-1 sp and in next dc, (ch 1, dc in next dc) 7 times, dc in next ch-1 sp and in next 15 dc, ch 1, skip next dc, (dc in next dc, ch 1) twice, dc in next 3 dc, ch 1, (dc in next dc, ch 1) twice, skip next dc, dc in next 15 dc and in next ch-1 sp, (dc in next dc, ch 1) 7 times, dc in next dc and in next ch-1 sp, (dc in next dc, ch 1) 4 times †, dc in next 3 dc, repeat from † to † once, dc in last 5 dc: 143 dc and 56 ch-1 sps.

Row 33: Ch 3, turn; dc in next 4 dc, † (ch 1, dc in next dc) 3 times, dc in next ch-1 sp, dc in next 3 dc and in next ch-1 sp, (dc in next dc, ch 1) 5 times, dc in next dc and in next ch-1 sp, (dc in next 7 dc, ch 1, skip next dc) twice, (dc in next dc, ch 1) 3 times, dc in next 3 dc, (ch 1, dc in next dc) 3 times, (ch 1, skip next dc, dc in next 7 dc) twice, dc in next ch-1 sp, (dc in next dc, ch 1) 5 times, dc in next dc and in next ch-1 sp, dc in next 3 dc and in next ch-1 sp, (dc in next dc, ch 1) 3 times †, dc in next 3 dc, repeat from † to † once, dc in last 5 dc: 147 dc and 52 ch-1 sps.

Row 34: Ch 3, turn; dc in next 4 dc, † (ch 1, dc in next dc) twice, dc in next ch-1 sp and in next 7 dc, dc in next ch-1 sp and in next dc, (ch 1, dc in next dc) 3 times, dc in next ch-1 sp and in next 7 dc, ch 1, skip next dc, dc in next dc, dc in next ch-1 sp and in next 7 dc, ch 1, (dc in next dc, ch 1) 3 times, dc in next 3 dc, ch 1, (dc in next dc, ch 1) 3 times, dc in next 7 dc, dc in next ch-1 sp and in next dc, ch 1, skip next dc, dc in next 7 dc and in next ch-1 sp, (dc in next dc, ch 1) 3 times, dc in next dc and in next ch-1 sp, dc in next 7 dc and in next ch-1 sp, (dc in next dc, ch 1) twice †, dc in next 3 dc, repeat from † to † once, dc in last 5 dc: 159 dc and 40 ch-1 sps.

Row 35: Ch 3, turn; dc in next 4 dc, † ch 1, dc in next dc and in next ch-1 sp, dc in next 11 dc and in next ch-1 sp, (dc in next dc, ch 1) twice, dc in next 7 dc, ch 1, skip next dc, dc in next dc, dc in next ch-1 sp and in next 7 dc, ch 1, skip next dc, (dc in next dc, ch 1) 4 times, dc in next 3 dc, ch 1, (dc in next dc, ch 1) 4 times, skip next dc, dc in next 7 dc, dc in next ch-1 sp and in next dc, ch 1, skip next dc, dc in next 7 dc, (ch 1, dc in next dc) twice, dc in next ch-1 sp and in next 11 dc, dc in next ch-1 sp and in next dc, ch 1 †, dc in next 3 dc, repeat from † to † once, dc in last 5 dc: 163 dc and 36 ch-1 sps.

Row 36: Ch 3, turn; dc in next 4 dc, † ch 1, dc in next 15 dc, ch 1, dc in next dc, ch 1, dc in next 5 dc, ch 1, skip next dc, dc in next dc, dc in next ch-1 sp and in next 7 dc, ch 1, skip next dc, (dc in next dc, ch 1) 5 times, dc in next 3 dc, ch 1, (dc in next dc, ch 1) 5 times, skip next dc, dc in next 7 dc, dc in next ch-1 sp and in next dc, ch 1, skip next dc, dc in next 5 dc, ch 1, dc in next dc, ch 1, dc in next 15 dc, ch 1 †, dc in next 3 dc, repeat from † to † once, dc in last 5 dc: 159 dc and 40 ch-1 sps.

Row 37: Ch 3, turn; dc in next 4 dc, † ch 1, dc in next 15 dc, (ch 1, dc in next dc) twice, (ch 1, skip next dc, dc in next dc) twice, dc in next ch-1 sp and in next 7 dc, ch 1, skip next dc, (dc in next dc, ch 1) 6 times, dc in next 3 dc, ch 1, (dc in next dc, ch 1) 6 times, skip next dc, dc in next 7 dc, dc in next ch-1 sp and in next dc, ch 1, (skip next dc, dc in next dc, ch 1) twice, dc in next dc, ch 1, dc in next 15 dc, ch 1 †, dc in next 3 dc, repeat from † to † once, dc in last 5 dc: 151 dc and 48 ch-1 sps.

Row 38: Ch 3, turn; dc in next 4 dc, † ch 1, dc in next 7 dc, ch 1, skip next dc, dc in next 7 dc, ch 1, (dc in next dc, ch 1) 3 times, dc in next 7 dc, ch 1, skip next dc, (dc in next dc, ch 1) 7 times, dc in next 3 dc, ch 1, (dc in next dc, ch 1) 7 times, skip next dc, dc in next 7 dc, ch 1, (dc in next dc, ch 1) 3 times, dc in next 7 dc, ch 1, skip next dc, dc in next 7 dc, ch 1 †, dc in next 3 dc, repeat from † to † once, dc in last 5 dc: 143 dc and 56 ch-1 sps.

Row 39: Ch 3, turn; dc in next 4 dc, † ch 1, [dc in next dc, ch 1, (skip next dc, dc in next dc, ch 1) 3 times] twice, (dc in next dc, ch 1) 4 times, (skip next dc, dc in next dc, ch 1) 3 times, (dc in next dc, ch 1) 7 times, dc in next 3 dc, ch 1, (dc in next dc, ch 1) 8 times, (skip next dc, dc in next dc, ch 1) 3 times, (dc in next dc, ch 1) 4 times, (skip next dc, dc in next dc, ch 1) 3 times, dc in next dc, ch 1, (skip next dc, dc in next dc, ch 1) 3 times †, dc in next 3 dc, repeat from † to † once, dc in last 5 dc: 107 dc and 92 ch-1 sps.

Row 40: Ch 3, turn; dc in next dc and in each dc and each ch-1 sp across: 199 dc.

Rows 41-128: Repeat Rows 3-40 twice, then repeat Rows 3-14 once **more**.

Row 129: Ch 3, turn; dc in next dc and in each dc across; finish off.

BLUE DELFT

Created to resemble beautiful china dishes, our thick and cuddly afghan is the perfect addition to your reading chair. Worked in blue and ecru worsted weight yarn, this cozy wrap will ward off chilly spring breezes.

Finished Size: 49" x 72"

MATERIALS
Worsted Weight Yarn:
Ecru - 34 ounces, (970 grams, 2,235 yards)
Blue - 15 ounces, (430 grams, 985 yards)
Crochet hook, size I (5.50 mm) **or** size needed for gauge
Yarn needle

GAUGE: One Square = 5 ³/₄"

STITCH GUIDE

CLUSTER
Ch 4, YO twice, insert hook in fourth ch from hook, YO and pull up a loop, (YO and draw through 2 loops on hook) twice, YO twice, insert hook in **same** ch, YO and pull up a loop, (YO and draw through 2 loops on hook) twice, YO and draw through all 3 loops on hook *(Figs. 11a & b, page 139)*.

SQUARE (Make 96)

Rnd 1 (Right side): With Blue, ch 6, (dc, ch 2) 7 times in sixth ch from hook; join with slip st to fourth ch of beginning ch-6: 8 ch-2 sps.
Note: Mark Rnd 1 as **right** side.
Rnd 2: Ch 1, turn; sc in same st, ch 3, (sc in next dc, ch 3) around; join with slip st to first sc, finish off: 8 ch-3 sps.
Rnd 3: With **right** side facing, join Ecru with sc in any sc *(see Joining With Sc, page 140)*; ch 1, working **behind** next ch-3 *(Fig. 16, page 141)*, dc in next ch-2 sp on Rnd 1, ch 1, ★ sc in next sc, ch 1, working **behind** next ch-3, dc in next ch-2 sp on Rnd 1, ch 1; repeat from ★ around; join with slip st to first sc, finish off: 16 sts.
Rnd 4: With **wrong** side facing, join Blue with sc in any sc; ch 2, sc in next dc, ch 2, ★ sc in next sc, ch 2, sc in next dc, ch 2; repeat from ★ around; join with slip st to first sc, finish off: 16 ch-2 sps.

Rnd 5: With **right** side facing, join Ecru with sc in any sc; working **behind** next ch-2, dc in next ch-1 sp on Rnd 3, ★ sc in next sc, working **behind** next ch-2, dc in next ch-1 sp on Rnd 3; repeat from ★ around; join with slip st in first sc: 32 sts.
Rnd 6: Ch 1, do **not** turn; sc in same st and in next 2 sts, ★ † hdc in next st, 2 dc in next st, (tr, ch 3, tr) in next st (corner made), 2 dc in next st, hdc in next st †, sc in next 3 sts; repeat from ★ 2 times **more**, then repeat from † to † once; join with slip st to first sc: 44 sts.
Rnd 7: Slip st in next sc, ch 1, sc in same st, ch 1, skip next st, (sc in next st, ch 1, skip next st) twice, (sc, ch 3, sc) in next corner ch-3 sp, ch 1, skip next st, ★ (sc in next st, ch 1, skip next st) 5 times, (sc, ch 3, sc) in next corner ch-3 sp, ch 1, skip next st; repeat from ★ 2 times **more**, (sc in next st, ch 1, skip next st) twice; join with slip st to first sc, finish off.
Rnd 8: With **wrong** side facing, join Blue with sc in first sc after any corner ch-3 sp; (ch 2, sc in next sc) 6 times, work Cluster, ★ sc in next sc, (ch 2, sc in next sc) 6 times, work Cluster; repeat from ★ around; join with slip st to first sc, finish off: 4 Clusters and 28 sc.
Rnd 9: With **right** side facing, join Ecru with sc in first sc after any corner Cluster; (working **behind** next ch-2, dc in next ch-1 sp on Rnd 7, sc in next sc) 6 times, working **behind** next Cluster, (2 dc, ch 3, 2 dc) in next ch-3 sp on Rnd 7, ★ sc in next sc, (working **behind** next ch-2, dc in next ch-1 sp on Rnd 7, sc in next sc) 6 times, working **behind** next Cluster, (2 dc, ch 3, 2 dc) in next ch-3 sp on Rnd 7; repeat from ★ around; join with slip st to first sc, finish off.

JOINING

Afghan is assembled by joining Squares into 8 vertical strips of 12 Squares each, and then by joining strips in same manner.

With **wrong** sides together, using Ecru and working through **both** loops, whipstitch Squares together *(Fig. 20b, page 142)*, working from center ch of one corner ch-3 to center ch of next corner ch-3.

Continued on page 28.

EDGING

Rnd 1: With **right** side facing, join Ecru with sc in any corner ch-3 sp; ch 3, sc in same sp, ★ † ch 1, skip next st, (sc in next st, ch 1, skip next st) 8 times, [(sc in next ch-sp, ch 1) twice, skip next st, (sc in next st, ch 1, skip next st) 8 times] across to next corner ch-3 sp †, (sc, ch 3, sc) in corner; repeat from ★ 2 times **more**, then repeat from † to † once; join with slip st to first sc.

Rnd 2: Ch 1, ★ (sc, ch 3, sc) in next corner, ch 1, (sc in next ch-1 sp, ch 1) across to next corner ch-3 sp; repeat from ★ around; join with slip st to first sc, finish off.

Rnd 3: With **wrong** side facing, join Blue with sc in first sc after any corner ch-3 sp; (ch 2, sc in next sc) across to next corner ch-3 sp, work Cluster, ★ sc in next sc, (ch 2, sc in next sc) across to next corner ch-3 sp, work Cluster; repeat from ★ around; join with slip st to first sc, finish off.

Rnd 4: With **right** side facing, join Ecru with sc in first sc after any corner Cluster; (working **behind** next ch-2, dc in next ch-1 sp on Rnd 2, sc in next sc) across to next Cluster, working **behind** Cluster, (2 dc, ch 3, 2 dc) in next ch-3 sp on Rnd 2, ★ sc in next sc, (working **behind** next ch-2, dc in next ch-1 sp on Rnd 2, sc in next sc) across to next Cluster, working **behind** Cluster, (2 dc, ch 3, 2 dc) in next ch-3 sp on Rnd 2; repeat from ★ around; join with slip st to first sc.

Rnd 5: Slip st in next st, ch 1, sc in same st, ch 1, skip next st, ★ (sc in next st, ch 1, skip next st) across to next corner ch-3 sp, (sc, ch 3, sc) in corner, ch 1, skip next st; repeat from ★ 3 times **more**, sc in next st, ch 1, skip next st; join with slip st to first sc.

Rnd 6: ★ (Slip st in next ch-1 sp, ch 1) across to next corner ch-3 sp, (slip st, ch 1) twice in corner; repeat from ★ 3 times **more**, (slip st in next ch-1 sp, ch 1) twice; join with slip st to first slip st, finish off.

A PRETTY WELCOME

Friends will feel welcome in your home when you lay out this beautiful afghan. Its pretty pattern spotlights the pineapple, a traditional symbol of hospitality.

Finished Size: 50" x 67"

MATERIALS
Worsted Weight Yarn:
   44 ounces, (1,250 grams, 2,230 yards)
Crochet hook, size H (5.00 mm) **or** size needed for gauge

GAUGE: Rows 2-13 of Afghan Body = 7"

Gauge Swatch: $5^3/_4$"w x $4^1/_2$"h
Work same as Bottom Point, page 29.

STITCH GUIDE

> **BEGINNING SHELL**
> Turn; skip first dc, slip st in next dc and in next ch-2 sp, ch 3, (dc, ch 2, 2 dc) in same sp.
> **SHELL**
> (2 Dc, ch 2, 2 dc) in sp indicated.
> **BOTTOM DECREASE** (uses 4 rows)
> YO, insert hook in same row, YO and pull up a loop, YO and draw through 2 loops on hook, YO, skip next 2 rows, insert hook in next row, YO and pull up a loop, YO and draw through 2 loops on hook, YO and draw through all 3 loops on hook.
> **TOP DECREASE** (uses 2 rows and 4 dc)
> YO, insert hook in same row, YO and pull up a loop, YO and draw through 2 loops on hook, YO, skip next 4 dc, insert hook in next row, YO and pull up a loop, YO and draw through 2 loops on hook, YO and draw through all 3 loops on hook.
> **CLUSTER** (uses one dc or one ch-1 sp)
> (Slip st, ch 2, dc) in dc or ch-1 sp indicated.

BOTTOM POINT (Make 7)

Ch 4; join with slip st to form a ring.

Row 1: Ch 3 **(counts as first dc, now and throughout)**, dc in ring, (ch 2, 2 dc in ring) twice: 6 dc and 2 ch-2 sps.

Row 2 (Right side): Work Beginning Shell, ch 1, work Shell in last ch-2 sp: 8 dc and 3 sps.

Note: Mark Row 2 as **right** side.

Row 3: Work Beginning Shell, ch 1, dc in next ch-1 sp, ch 1, work Shell in last ch-2 sp: 9 dc and 4 sps.

Row 4: Work Beginning Shell, ch 1, skip next ch-1 sp, (dc, ch 3, dc) in next dc, ch 1, skip next ch-1 sp, work Shell in last ch-2 sp: 10 dc and 5 sps.

Row 5: Work Beginning Shell, ch 1, skip next ch-1 sp, 7 dc in next ch-3 sp, ch 1, skip next ch-1 sp, work Shell in last ch-2 sp: 15 dc and 4 sps.

Row 6: Work Beginning Shell, ch 1, skip next ch-1 sp, (hdc in next dc, ch 1) 7 times, skip next ch-1 sp, work Shell in last ch-2 sp; finish off: 10 sps.

LAST BOTTOM POINT

Work same as Bottom Point through Row 6; do **not** finish off: 10 sps.

AFGHAN BODY

Row 1 (Joining row): Work Beginning Shell, ch 2, skip next ch-1 sp, (sc in next ch-1 sp, ch 2) 6 times, skip next ch-1 sp, work Shell in last ch-2 sp; ★ with **wrong** side of next Bottom Point facing and working in sps across Row 6, work Shell in first ch-2 sp, ch 2, skip next ch-1 sp, (sc in next ch-1 sp, ch 2) 6 times, skip next ch-1 sp, work Shell in last ch-2 sp; repeat from ★ 6 times **more**: 72 ch-2 sps.

Row 2: Work Beginning Shell, ★ † ch 2, skip next ch-2 sp, (sc in next ch-2 sp, ch 2) 5 times, skip next ch-2 sp, work Shell in next ch-2 sp †, ch 1, work Shell in next ch-2 sp; repeat from ★ 6 times **more**, then repeat from † to † once: 71 sps.

Row 3: Work Beginning Shell, ★ † ch 2, skip next ch-2 sp, (sc in next ch-2 sp, ch 2) 4 times, skip next ch-2 sp, work Shell in next ch-2 sp †, ch 1, dc in next ch-1 sp, ch 1, work Shell in next ch-2 sp; repeat from ★ 6 times **more**, then repeat from † to † once: 70 sps.

Row 4: Work Beginning Shell, ★ † ch 2, skip next ch-2 sp, (sc in next ch-2 sp, ch 2) 3 times, skip next ch-2 sp, work Shell in next ch-2 sp †, ch 1, skip next ch-1 sp, (dc, ch 3, dc) in next dc, ch 1, skip next ch-1 sp, work Shell in next ch-2 sp; repeat from ★ 6 times **more**, then repeat from † to † once: 69 sps.

Row 5: Work Beginning Shell, ★ † ch 2, skip next ch-2 sp, (sc in next ch-2 sp, ch 2) twice, skip next ch-2 sp, work Shell in next ch-2 sp †, ch 1, skip next ch-1 sp, 7 dc in next ch-3 sp, ch 1, skip next ch-1 sp, work Shell in next ch-2 sp; repeat from ★ 6 times **more**, then repeat from † to † once: 54 sps.

Row 6: Work Beginning Shell, ★ † ch 2, skip next ch-2 sp, sc in next ch-2 sp, ch 2, skip next ch-2 sp, work Shell in next ch-2 sp †, ch 1, skip next ch-1 sp, (hdc in next dc, ch 1) 7 times, skip next ch-1 sp, work Shell in next ch-2 sp; repeat from ★ 6 times **more**, then repeat from † to † once: 88 sps.

Row 7: Work Beginning Shell, skip next 2 ch-2 sps, work Shell in next ch-2 sp, ★ ch 2, skip next ch-1 sp, (sc in next ch-1 sp, ch 2) 6 times, skip next ch-1 sp, work Shell in next ch-2 sp, skip next 2 ch-2 sps, work Shell in next ch-2 sp; repeat from ★ across: 65 ch-2 sps.

Row 8: Work Beginning Shell, ch 1, work Shell in next ch-2 sp, ★ ch 2, skip next ch-2 sp, (sc in next ch-2 sp, ch 2) 5 times, skip next ch-2 sp, work Shell in next ch-2 sp, ch 1, work Shell in next ch-2 sp; repeat from ★ across: 66 sps.

Row 9: Work Beginning Shell, ch 1, dc in next ch-1 sp, ch 1, work Shell in next ch-2 sp, ★ ch 2, skip next ch-2 sp, (sc in next ch-2 sp, ch 2) 4 times, skip next ch-2 sp, work Shell in next ch-2 sp, ch 1, dc in next ch-1 sp, ch 1, work Shell in next ch-2 sp; repeat from ★ across: 67 sps.

Row 10: Work Beginning Shell, ch 1, skip next ch-1 sp, (dc, ch 3, dc) in next dc, ch 1, skip next ch-1 sp, work Shell in next ch-2 sp, ★ ch 2, skip next ch-2 sp, (sc in next ch-2 sp, ch 2) 3 times, skip next ch-2 sp, work Shell in next ch-2 sp, ch 1, skip next ch-1 sp, (dc, ch 3, dc) in next dc, ch 1, skip next ch-1 sp, work Shell in next ch-2 sp; repeat from ★ across: 68 sps.

Row 11: Work Beginning Shell, ch 1, skip next ch-1 sp, 7 dc in next ch-3 sp, ch 1, skip next ch-1 sp, work Shell in next ch-2 sp, ★ ch 2, skip next ch-2 sp, (sc in next ch-2 sp, ch 2) twice, skip next ch-2 sp, work Shell in next ch-2 sp, ch 1, skip next ch-1 sp, 7 dc in next ch-3 sp, ch 1, skip next ch-1 sp, work Shell in next ch-2 sp; repeat from ★ across: 53 sps.

Row 12: Work Beginning Shell, ch 1, skip next ch-1 sp, (hdc in next dc, ch 1) 7 times, skip next ch-1 sp, work Shell in next ch-2 sp, ★ ch 2, skip next ch-2 sp, sc in next ch-2 sp, ch 2, skip next ch-2 sp, work Shell in next ch-2 sp, ch 1, skip next ch-1 sp, (hdc in next dc, ch 1) 7 times, skip next ch-1 sp, work Shell in next ch-2 sp; repeat from ★ across; do **not** finish off: 94 sps.

Continued on page 30.

Row 13: Work Beginning Shell, ★ † ch 2, skip next ch-1 sp, (sc in next ch-1 sp, ch 2) 6 times, skip next ch-1 sp, work Shell in next ch-2 sp †, skip next 2 ch-2 sps, work Shell in next ch-2 sp; repeat from ★ 6 times **more**, then repeat from † to † once: 72 ch-2 sps.

Rows 14-97: Repeat Rows 2-13, 7 times; do **not** finish off: 72 ch-2 sps.

FIRST TOP POINT

Row 1: Work Beginning Shell, ch 2, skip next ch-2 sp, (sc in next ch-2 sp, ch 2) 5 times, skip next ch-2 sp, work Shell in next ch-2 sp, leave remaining sts unworked: 8 ch-2 sps.

Row 2: Work Beginning Shell, ch 2, skip next ch-2 sp, (sc in next ch-2 sp, ch 2) 4 times, skip next ch-2 sp, work Shell in last ch-2 sp: 7 ch-2 sps.

Row 3: Work Beginning Shell, ch 2, skip next ch-2 sp, (sc in next ch-2 sp, ch 2) 3 times, skip next ch-2 sp, work Shell in last ch-2 sp: 6 ch-2 sps.

Row 4: Work Beginning Shell, ch 2, skip next ch-2 sp, (sc in next ch-2 sp, ch 2) twice, skip next ch-2 sp, work Shell in last ch-2 sp: 5 ch-2 sps.

Row 5: Work Beginning Shell, ch 2, skip next ch-2 sp, sc in next ch-2 sp, ch 2, skip next ch-2 sp, work Shell in last ch-2 sp: 4 ch-2 sps.

Row 6: Work Beginning Shell, skip next 2 ch-2 sps, work Shell in last ch-2 sp: 2 ch-2 sps.

Row 7: Turn; skip first dc, slip st in next dc and in next ch-2 sp; ch 3, YO, insert hook in same sp, YO and pull up a loop, YO and draw through 2 loops on hook, YO, insert hook in next ch-2 sp, YO and pull up a loop, YO and draw through 2 loops on hook, YO and draw through all 3 loops on hook, dc in same sp; finish off: 3 sts.

NEXT 7 TOP POINTS

Row 1: With **right** side facing, join yarn with slip st in next unworked ch-2 sp on Row 97; ch 3, (dc, ch 2, 2 dc) in same sp, ch 2, skip next ch-2 sp, (sc in next ch-2 sp, ch 2) 5 times, skip next ch-2 sp, work Shell in next ch-2 sp, leave remaining sts unworked: 8 ch-2 sps.

Rows 2-7: Work same as First Top Point; at end of last Top Point, do **not** finish off: 3 sts.

EDGING

Rnd 1: Do **not** turn; working in end of rows, (slip st, ch 3, dc) in first row, † 2 dc in each of next 6 rows, dc in next row, (ch 1, dc in same row) twice, [2 dc in each of next 4 rows, dc in next 3 rows, 2 dc in each of next 4 rows, dc in next row, (ch 1, dc in same row) twice] 8 times †, 2 dc in each of next 6 rows, dc in beginning ring, (ch 1, dc in same ring) twice, ★ 2 dc in each of next 5 rows, dc in next row, work Bottom Decrease, dc in same row, 2 dc in each of next 5 rows, dc in beginning ring, (ch 1, dc in same ring) twice; repeat from ★ 6 times **more**, then repeat from † to † once, 2 dc in each of next 7 rows, skip first dc on Row 7 of Top Point, dc in next st, (ch 1, dc in same st) twice, ♥ 2 dc in same row and in each of next 5 rows, dc in next row, work Top Decrease, dc in same row, 2 dc in each of next 6 rows, skip first dc on Row 7 of Top Point, dc in next st, (ch 1, dc in same st) twice ♥; repeat from ♥ to ♥ across; join with slip st to first dc: 808 sts.

Rnd 2: Ch 2, dc in same st, (skip next dc, work Cluster in next dc) 7 times, (skip next ch-1 sp, work Cluster in next dc) twice, [(skip next dc, work Cluster in next dc) 3 times, skip next dc, slip st in next 2 dc, work Cluster in next dc, (skip next dc, work Cluster in next dc) 5 times, (skip next ch-1 sp, work Cluster in next dc) twice] 8 times, (skip next dc, work Cluster in next dc) 6 times, (skip next dc, work Cluster in next ch-1 sp) twice, [(skip next dc, work Cluster in next dc) 5 times, (skip next st, slip st in next dc) twice, (skip next dc, work Cluster in next dc) 5 times, (skip next dc, work Cluster in next ch-1 sp) twice] 7 times, (skip next dc, work Cluster in next dc) 7 times, (skip next ch-1 sp, work Cluster in next dc) twice, [(skip next dc, work Cluster in next dc) 4 times, skip next dc, slip st in next 2 dc, work Cluster in next dc, (skip next dc, work Cluster in next dc) 4 times, (skip next ch-1 sp, work Cluster in next dc) twice] 8 times, (skip next dc, work Cluster in next dc) 7 times, (skip next dc, work Cluster in next ch-1 sp) twice, [(skip next dc, work Cluster in next dc) 6 times, (skip next st, slip st in next dc) twice, (skip next dc, work Cluster in next dc) 6 times, (skip next dc, work Cluster in next ch-1 sp) twice] 7 times, skip last dc; join with slip st at base of beginning ch-2, finish off.

STORY TIME

*Warm and snuggly in the softest sport weight yarn, this glorious afghan
is like a burst of sunshine. Clusters create a tender, lacy look
that's lovely for a new mother or a special friend.*

Finished Size: 35" x 47"

MATERIALS
Sport Weight Yarn:
   19 ounces, (540 grams, 1,520 yards)
Crochet hook, size H (5.00 mm) **or** size needed
   for gauge

GAUGE: In pattern, 2 repeats = 4"; 8 rows = 4¹/₄"

Gauge Swatch: 4¹/₄" square
Ch 20 **loosely**.
Work same as Afghan Body for 8 rows.
Finish off.

STITCH GUIDE

BEGINNING CLUSTER (uses one st or sp)
Ch 2, ★ YO, insert hook in st or sp indicated, YO
and pull up a loop, YO and draw through
2 loops on hook; repeat from ★ once **more**, YO
and draw through all 3 loops on hook (*Figs. 11a
& b, page 139*).

CLUSTER (uses one st or sp)
★ YO, insert hook in st or sp indicated, YO and
pull up a loop, YO and draw through 2 loops on
hook; repeat from ★ 2 times **more**, YO and draw
through all 4 loops on hook (*Figs. 11a & b,
page 139*).

PICOT
Ch 3, sc in top of dc just made.

AFGHAN BODY
Ch 128 **loosely**.
Row 1: Sc in second ch from hook, ch 3, skip next
3 chs, (sc in next ch, ch 3) twice, ★ (skip next 3 chs,
sc in next ch, ch 3) twice, sc in next ch, ch 3; repeat
from ★ across to last 4 chs, skip next 3 chs, sc in last
ch: 43 sc and 42 ch-3 sps.

Row 2 (Right side): Ch 4 (**counts as first dc plus
ch 1, now and throughout**), turn; skip next ch-3 sp,
(2 dc, ch 2, 2 dc) in next ch-3 sp, ch 1, skip next
ch-3 sp, ★ work Cluster in next sc, ch 1, skip next
ch-3 sp, (2 dc, ch 2, 2 dc) in next ch-3 sp, ch 1, skip
next ch-3 sp; repeat from ★ across to last sc, dc in
last sc: 13 Clusters and 42 sps.
Row 3: Ch 1, turn; sc in first dc, ch 3, skip next
ch-1 sp, (sc, ch 3) twice in next ch-2 sp, ★ sc in next
Cluster, ch 3, skip next ch-1 sp, (sc, ch 3) twice in
next ch-2 sp; repeat from ★ across to last 3 dc, skip
next 2 dc, sc in last dc: 43 sc and 42 ch-3 sps.
Row 4: Ch 4, turn; skip next ch-3 sp, (2 dc, ch 2,
2 dc) in next ch-3 sp, ch 1, skip next ch-3 sp, ★ work
Cluster in next sc, ch 1, skip next ch-3 sp, (2 dc, ch 2,
2 dc) in next ch-3 sp, ch 1, skip next ch-3 sp; repeat
from ★ across to last sc, dc in last sc: 13 Clusters and
42 sps.
Rows 5-78: Repeat Rows 3 and 4, 37 times.
Row 79: Ch 1, turn; sc in first dc, ch 3, skip next
ch-1 sp, sc in next ch-2 sp, ch 3, ★ sc in next Cluster,
ch 3, skip next ch-1 sp, sc in next ch-2 sp, ch 3;
repeat from ★ across to last 3 dc, skip next 2 dc, sc in
last dc; do **not** finish off: 28 ch-3 sps.

EDGING
Rnd 1: Ch 1, turn; sc in first sc, 2 sc in next ch-3 sp,
3 sc in each ch-3 sp across, sc in last sc, place marker
around sc just made for st placement; † working in
end of rows, sc in first row, (2 sc in next row, sc in
next row) across to last 2 rows, 3 sc in next row, sc in
last row †; working in free loops (*Fig. 15b, page 140*)
and in sps across beginning ch, sc in ch at base of
first sc, place marker around sc just made for st
placement, 2 sc in next sp, sc in sp **between** next
2 sc, 2 sc in next sp, ★ sc in next ch, 2 sc in next sp,
sc in sp **between** next 2 sc, 2 sc in next sp; repeat
from ★ across, sc in last ch, place marker around sc
just made for st placement; repeat from † to † once;
join with slip st to first sc: 408 sc.

Continued on page 34.

Rnd 2: Do **not** turn; work (Beginning Cluster, ch 5, Cluster) in same st, ch 3, skip next 2 sc, sc in next sc, (ch 5, skip next 2 sc, sc in next sc) twice, ch 3, ★ † YO twice, skip next 2 sc, insert hook in next sc, YO and pull up a loop, (YO and draw through 2 loops on hook twice), (YO, insert hook in **same** st, YO and pull up a loop, YO and draw through 2 loops on hook) twice, YO and draw through all 4 loops on hook, ch 3, skip next 2 sc, sc in next sc, (ch 5, skip next 2 sc, sc in next sc) twice, ch 3 †, repeat from † to † across to within 2 sc of next marked sc, skip next 2 sc, work (Cluster, ch 5, Cluster) in marked sc, ch 3, skip next 2 sc, sc in next sc, (ch 5, skip next 2 sc, sc in next sc) twice, ch 3; repeat from ★ 2 times **more**, then repeat from † to † across; join with slip st to top of Beginning Cluster: 140 sps.

Rnd 3: Slip st in first ch-5 sp, ch 5 **(counts as first tr plus ch 1)**, [tr, (ch 1, tr) 6 times] in same sp, ★ † ch 2, skip next ch-3 sp, sc in next ch-5 sp, ch 3, sc in next ch-5 sp, ch 2, skip next ch-3 sp, [tr in next st, (ch 1, tr in same st) 6 times, ch 2, skip next ch-3 sp, sc in next ch-5 sp, ch 3, sc in next ch-5 sp, ch 2, skip next ch-3 sp] across to next corner ch-5 sp †, [tr, (ch 1, tr) 7 times] in corner ch-5 sp; repeat from ★ 2 times **more**, then repeat from † to † once; join with slip st to first tr: 310 sps.

Rnd 4: Slip st in first ch-1 sp, work Beginning Cluster in same sp, ch 3, [(work Cluster in next ch-1 sp, ch 3) 6 times, skip next ch-2 sp, sc in next ch-3 sp, ch 3, skip next ch-2 sp] across to next corner tr group, ★ (work Cluster in next ch-1 sp, ch 3) 7 times, skip next ch-2 sp, sc in next ch-3 sp, ch 3, skip next ch-2 sp, [(work Cluster in next ch-1 sp, ch 3) 6 times, skip next ch-2 sp, sc in next ch-3 sp, ch 3, skip next ch-2 sp] across to next corner tr group; repeat from ★ 2 times **more**; join with slip st to top of Beginning Cluster: 242 ch-3 sps.

Rnd 5: [Slip st, ch 6, sc in fourth ch from hook, dc] in first ch-3 sp, ★ † (work Picot, dc) twice in each of next 5 ch-3 sps, ch 1, skip next ch-3 sp, slip st in next sc, ch 1, skip next ch-3 sp, [(dc, work Picot, dc) in next ch-3 sp, (work Picot, dc) twice in each of next 4 ch-3 sps, ch 1, skip next ch-3 sp, slip st in next sc, ch 1, skip next ch-3 sp] across to next corner 7-Cluster group †, (dc, work Picot, dc) in next ch-3 sp; repeat from ★ 2 times **more**, then repeat from † to † once; join with slip st to third ch of beginning ch-6, finish off.

FORGET-ME-NOT BOUQUET

Like a field of forget-me-nots, our intense blue throw will bring beauty to your home. The flower motifs are picturesquely assembled to create interest at the edges.

Finished Size: 43" x 60"

MATERIALS
Worsted Weight Brushed Acrylic Yarn:
   Blue - 37 ounces, (1,050 grams, 2,855 yards)
   Yellow - 6 ounces, (170 grams, 465 yards)
Crochet hook, size I (5.50 mm) **or** size needed for gauge

GAUGE: Each Flower = 4"

FIRST FLOWER

With Yellow, ch 5; join with slip st to form a ring.
Rnd 1 (Right side): Ch 1, 18 sc in ring; join with slip st to first sc, finish off.
Note: Mark Rnd 1 as **right** side.

Rnd 2: With **right** side facing, join Blue with slip st in any sc; [(sc, dc, tr) in next sc, (tr, dc, sc) in next sc **(Petal made)**], ★ slip st in next sc, (sc, dc, tr) in next sc, (tr, dc, sc) in next sc; repeat from ★ around; join with slip st to first slip st: 6 Petals.

Rnd 3: Ch 3, working **behind** Petals, ★ slip st around post of slip st **between** next 2 Petals, ch 3; repeat from ★ around; join with slip st to base of beginning ch-3: 6 ch-3 sps.

Rnd 4: Slip st in first ch-3 sp, ch 5 **(counts as first dc plus ch 2)**, dc in same sp, ch 3, ★ (dc, ch 2, dc) in next ch-3 sp, ch 3; repeat from ★ around; join with slip st to first dc: 12 sps.

Continued on page 36.

Rnd 5: Slip st in first ch-2 sp, ch 3 **(counts as first dc, now and throughout)**, (3 dc, ch 1, 4 dc) in same sp, slip st in next ch-3 sp, ★ (4 dc, ch 1, 4 dc) in next ch-2 sp, slip st in next ch-3 sp; repeat from ★ around; join with slip st to first dc, finish off: 6 ch-1 sps.

ADDITIONAL FLOWERS

Work same as First Flower through Rnd 4; do **not** finish off: 12 sps.

Rnd 5: Work One, Two, or Three Side Joining **(Fig. 19, page 141)**, using Placement Diagram as a guide.

ONE SIDE JOINING

Slip st in first ch-2 sp, ch 3, 3 dc in same sp; holding Flowers with **wrong** sides together, slip st in corresponding ch-1 sp on **adjacent Flower**, 4 dc in same sp on **new Flower**, slip st in next ch-3 sp, 4 dc in next ch-2 sp, slip st in next ch-1 sp on **adjacent Flower**, 4 dc in same sp on **new Flower**, slip st in next ch-3 sp, ★ (4 dc, ch 1, 4 dc) in next ch-2 sp, slip st in next ch-3 sp; repeat from ★ around; join with slip st to first dc, finish off.

TWO SIDE JOINING

Slip st in first ch-2 sp, ch 3, 3 dc in same sp; holding Flowers with **wrong** sides together, slip st in corresponding ch-1 sp on **adjacent Flower**, 4 dc in same sp on **new Flower**, slip st in next ch-3 sp, ★ 4 dc in next ch-2 sp, slip st in next ch-1 sp on **adjacent Flower**, 4 dc in same sp on **new Flower**, slip st in next ch-3 sp; repeat from ★ once **more**, † (4 dc, ch 1, 4 dc) in next ch-2 sp, slip st in next ch-3 sp †, repeat from † to † around; join with slip st to first dc, finish off.

THREE SIDE JOINING

Slip st in first ch-2 sp, ch 3, 3 dc in same sp; holding Flowers with **wrong** sides together, slip st in corresponding ch-1 sp on **adjacent Flower**, 4 dc in same sp on **new Flower**, slip st in next ch-3 sp, ★ 4 dc in next ch-2 sp, slip st in next ch-1 sp on **adjacent Flower**, 4 dc in same sp on **new Flower**, slip st in next ch-3 sp; repeat from ★ 2 times **more**, † (4 dc, ch 1, 4 dc) in next ch-2 sp, slip st in next ch-3 sp †, repeat from † to † once **more**; join with slip st to first dc, finish off.

PLACEMENT DIAGRAM

NIGHTY-NIGHT GRANNY

Tuck Baby in for the night with this sweet afghan. Worked in strips, the granny square throw comes together easily for a great shower gift.

Finished Size: 36" x 46"

MATERIALS

Sport Weight Yarn:
  Green - 14$\frac{1}{2}$ ounces, (410 grams, 1,160 yards)
  White - 7$\frac{3}{4}$ ounces, (220 grams, 620 yards)
  Pink - 3$\frac{1}{2}$ ounces, (100 grams, 280 yards)
Crochet hook, size G (4.00 mm) **or** size needed
  for gauge
Yarn needle

GAUGE SWATCH: 2$\frac{1}{4}$"
Work same as Small Square.

STITCH GUIDE

SINGLE CROCHET DECREASE
  (abbreviated sc decrease) (uses next 2 sps)
Pull up a loop in next 2 sps, YO and draw
through all 3 loops on hook.
DOUBLE CROCHET DECREASE
  (abbreviated dc decrease) (uses next 2 sps)
★ YO, insert hook in **next** sp, YO and pull up a
loop, YO and draw through 2 loops on hook;
repeat from ★ once **more**, YO and draw through
all 3 loops on hook **(counts as one dc)**.

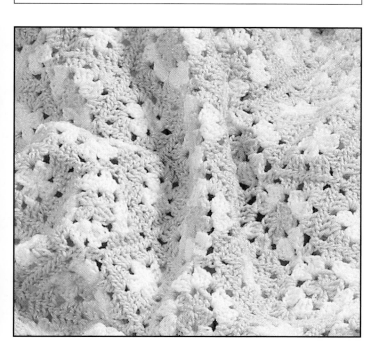

STRIP (Make 8)
FIRST SQUARE

Rnd 1 (Right side): With Pink, ch 4, 2 dc in fourth ch
from hook, ch 3, (3 dc in same ch, ch 3) 3 times; join
with slip st to top of beginning ch-4, finish off:
4 ch-3 sps.
Note: Mark Rnd 1 as **right** side.
Rnd 2: With **right** side facing, join White with slip st
in any ch-3 sp; ch 3 **(counts as first dc, now and
throughout)**, (2 dc, ch 3, 3 dc) in same sp, ch 1,
★ (3 dc, ch 3, 3 dc) in next ch-3 sp, ch 1; repeat from
★ 2 times **more**; join with slip st to first dc, finish off:
24 dc and 8 sps.

SECOND SQUARE

Rnd 1 (Right side): Work same as First Square:
4 ch-3 sps.
Note: Mark Rnd 1 as **right** side.
Rnd 2: With **right** side facing, join White with slip st
in any ch-3 sp; ch 3, 2 dc in same sp, ch 1, ★ (3 dc,
ch 3, 3 dc) in next ch-3 sp, ch 1; repeat from ★
2 times **more**, 3 dc in same sp as first dc, ch 1, drop
loop from hook, with **right** side of First Square
facing, insert hook in center ch of any corner ch-3,
hook dropped loop and draw through, ch 1; join
with slip st to first dc, finish off: 24 dc and 8 sps.

REMAINING 13 SQUARES

Rnd 1 (Right side): Work same as First Square:
4 ch-3 sps.
Note: Mark Rnd 1 as **right** side.
Rnd 2: With **right** side facing, join White with slip st
in any ch-3 sp; ch 3, 2 dc in same sp, ch 1, ★ (3 dc,
ch 3, 3 dc) in next ch-3 sp, ch 1; repeat from ★
2 times **more**, 3 dc in same sp as first dc, ch 1, drop
loop from hook, with **right** side of previous Square
facing, insert hook in center ch of corner opposite
previous joining, hook dropped loop and draw
through, ch 1; join with slip st to first dc, finish off:
24 dc and 8 sps.

Continued on page 38.

EDGING

Rnd 1: With **right** side facing and holding strip vertically, join Green with slip st in top ch-3 sp (opposite joining); ch 3, (2 dc, ch 3, 3 dc) in same sp, † ch 1, 3 dc in next ch-1 sp, ch 1, (3 dc, ch 3, 3 dc) in next ch-3 sp, ch 1, 3 dc in next ch-1 sp, ch 1, [dc decrease, ch 1, 3 dc in next ch-1 sp, ch 1, (3 dc, ch 3, 3 dc) in next ch-3 sp, ch 1, 3 dc in next ch-1 sp, ch 1] across to ch-3 sp at opposite point †, (3 dc, ch 3, 3 dc) in next ch-3 sp, repeat from † to † once; join with slip st to first dc, finish off: 400 dc and 152 sps.

SMALL SQUARE (Make 98)

Rnd 1 (Right side): With White, ch 4, 2 dc in fourth ch from hook, ch 3, (3 dc in same ch, ch 3) 3 times; join with slip st to top of beginning ch-4, finish off: 4 ch-3 sps.

Note: Mark Rnd 1 as **right** side.

Rnd 2: With **right** side facing, join Green with slip st in any ch-3 sp; ch 3, (2 dc, ch 3, 3 dc) in same sp, ch 1, ★ (3 dc, ch 3, 3 dc) in next ch-3 sp, ch 1; repeat from ★ 2 times **more**; join with slip st to first dc, finish off: 24 dc and 8 sps.

HALF SQUARE (Make 28)

Row 1: With Green, ch 6, place marker in second ch from hook for st placement, (3 dc, ch 3, 3 dc, ch 1, tr) in sixth ch from hook: 6 dc and 3 sps.

Row 2 (Right side): Ch 5, turn; 3 dc in first ch-1 sp, ch 1, (3 dc, ch 3, 3 dc) in next ch-3 sp, ch 1, 3 dc in next sp, ch 5, slip st in marked ch; finish off: 12 dc and 5 sps.

Note: Mark Row 2 as **right** side.

ASSEMBLY

With Green, using Placement Diagram as a guide, and working through **both** loops, ★ whipstitch 14 Small Squares to one Strip *(Fig. 20b, page 142)*, whipstitch next Strip to Small Squares; repeat from ★ 6 times **more**, then whipstitch Half Squares in place along each long edge.

BORDER

Rnd 1: With **right** side of short edge facing, join Green with sc in top right ch-3 sp (Point A) *(see Joining With Sc, page 140)*; ch 2, sc in same sp, † [ch 1, skip next dc, sc in next dc, ch 1, (sc in next ch-1 sp, ch 1, skip next dc, sc in next dc, ch 1) twice, sc decrease, ch 1, skip next dc, sc in next dc, ch 1, (sc in next ch-1 sp, ch 1, skip next dc, sc in next dc, ch 1) twice, (sc, ch 2, sc) in next ch-3 sp] 7 times, (ch 1, skip next dc, sc in next dc, ch 1, sc in next sp) 3 times, ch 2, (sc, ch 1) twice in next sp, sc in next sp, ch 1, sc in free loop of ch at center of Half Square *(Fig. 15b, page 140)*, ch 1, sc in next sp, [ch 1, (sc, ch 1) twice in each of next 2 sps, sc in next sp, ch 1, sc in free loop of ch at center of Half Square, ch 1, sc in next sp] 13 times, (ch 1, sc) twice in next sp, ch 2, (sc in next sp, ch 1, skip next dc, sc in next dc, ch 1) 3 times †, (sc, ch 2, sc) in next ch-3 sp, repeat from † to † once; join with slip st to first sc: 406 sps.

Rnd 2: Ch 1, (sc, ch 2, sc) in first ch-2 sp, † ch 1, [(sc in next ch-1 sp, ch 1) 5 times, sc decrease, ch 1, (sc in next ch-1 sp, ch 1) 5 times, (sc, ch 2, sc) in next ch-2 sp, ch 1] 7 times, (sc in next ch-1 sp, ch 1) 6 times, (sc, ch 1) twice in next ch-2 sp, (sc in next ch-1 sp, ch 1) across to next ch-2 sp, (sc, ch 1) twice in ch-2 sp, (sc in next ch-1 sp, ch 1) 6 times †, (sc, ch 2, sc) in next ch-2 sp, repeat from † to † once; join with slip st to first sc: 412 sps.

Rnd 3: Ch 1, (slip st, ch 3, slip st) in first ch-2 sp, † ch 1, [(slip st in next ch-1 sp, ch 1) 12 times, (slip st, ch 3, slip st) in next ch-2 sp, ch 1] 7 times, (slip st in next ch-1 sp, ch 1) across to next ch-2 sp †, (slip st, ch 3, slip st) in ch-2 sp, repeat from † to † once; join with slip st to first slip st, finish off.

PLACEMENT DIAGRAM

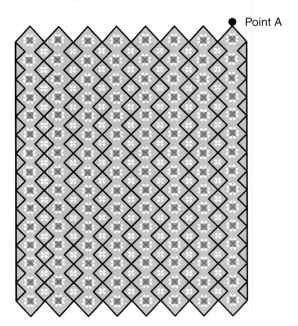

Point A

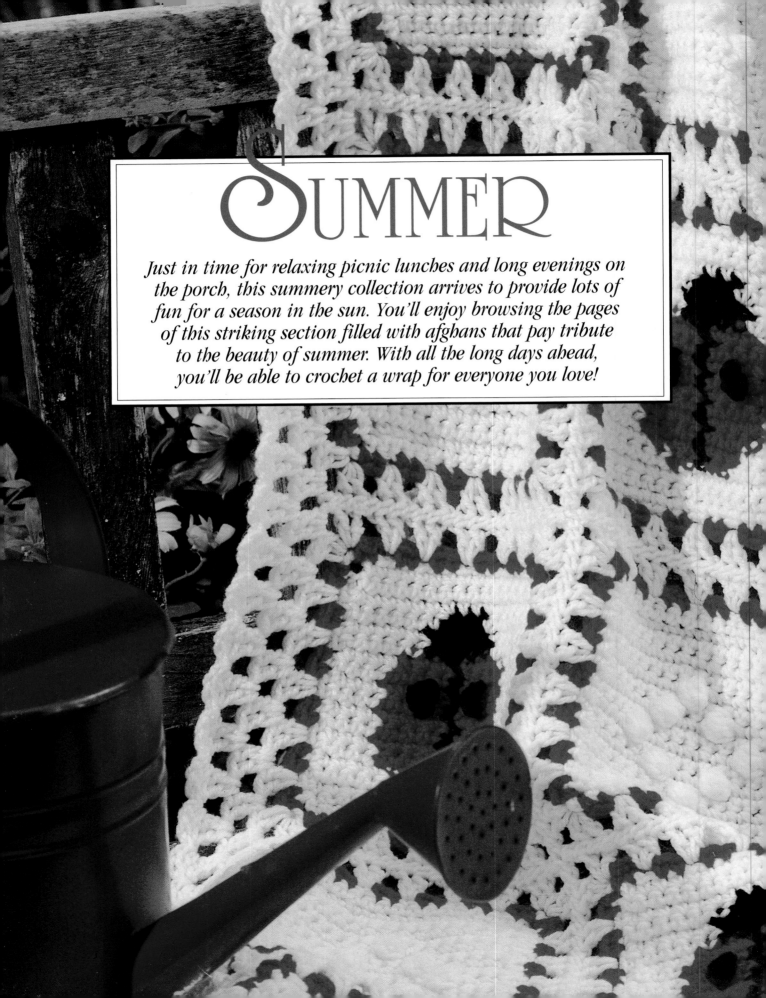

SUMMER

Just in time for relaxing picnic lunches and long evenings on the porch, this summery collection arrives to provide lots of fun for a season in the sun. You'll enjoy browsing the pages of this striking section filled with afghans that pay tribute to the beauty of summer. With all the long days ahead, you'll be able to crochet a wrap for everyone you love!

SUMMER MINT

With its fresh hue, this wispy throw will be an inviting part of your summer décor.
Stitched in bulky yarn, our luxurious afghan offers comfort for leisurely days.

Finished Size: 47" x 63"

MATERIALS
 Bulky Weight Brushed Acrylic Yarn:
  53 ounces, (1,510 grams, 2,385 yards)
 Crochet hook, size I (5.50 mm) **or** size needed
  for gauge

GAUGE: In pattern, 2 repeats and 7 rows = 4^1/$_2$"

Gauge Swatch: 5" square
Ch 21.
Work same as Afghan for 8 rows.
Finish off.

STITCH GUIDE

CLUSTER (uses next 5 dc)
★ YO, insert hook in **next** dc, YO and pull up a
loop, YO and draw through 2 loops on hook;
repeat from ★ 4 times **more**, YO and draw
through all 6 loops on hook (*Figs. 12a & b,
page 139*).
BEGINNING CLUSTER (uses first 3 dc)
Ch 2, turn; ★ YO, insert hook in **next** dc, YO and
pull up a loop, YO and draw through 2 loops on
hook; repeat from ★ once **more**, YO and draw
through all 3 loops on hook (*Figs. 12a & b,
page 139*).
ENDING CLUSTER (uses last 3 dc)
★ YO, insert hook in **next** dc, YO and pull up a
loop, YO and draw through 2 loops on hook;
repeat from ★ 2 times **more**, YO and draw
through all 4 loops on hook (*Figs. 12a & b,
page 139*).

AFGHAN
Ch 173.
Row 1: 5 Dc in ninth ch from hook, ch 2, skip next
3 chs, dc in next ch, ★ ch 2, skip next 3 chs, 5 dc in
next ch, ch 2, skip next 3 chs, dc in next ch; repeat
from ★ across: 126 dc.
Row 2 (Right side): Ch 6 **(counts as first dc plus
ch 3, now and throughout)**, turn; work Cluster, ch 3,
★ dc in next dc, ch 3, work Cluster, ch 3; repeat
from ★ across, skip next 2 chs, dc in next ch: 22 dc
and 21 Clusters.
Note: Mark Row 2 as **right** side.
Row 3: Ch 3 **(counts as first dc, now and
throughout)**, turn; 2 dc in same st, ch 2, dc in next
Cluster, ch 2, ★ 5 dc in next dc, ch 2, dc in next
Cluster, ch 2; repeat from ★ across to last dc, 3 dc in
last dc: 127 dc.
Row 4: Work Beginning Cluster, ch 3, dc in next dc,
ch 3, ★ work Cluster, ch 3, dc in next dc, ch 3; repeat
from ★ across to last 3 dc, work Ending Cluster:
21 dc and 22 Clusters.
Row 5: Ch 5 **(counts as first dc plus ch 2)**, turn; 5 dc
in next dc, ch 2, dc in next Cluster, ★ ch 2, 5 dc in
next dc, ch 2, dc in next Cluster; repeat from ★
across: 127 dc.
Row 6: Ch 6, turn; work Cluster, ch 3, dc in next dc,
★ ch 3, work Cluster, ch 3, dc in next dc; repeat from
★ across: 22 dc and 21 Clusters.
Repeat Rows 3-6 until Afghan measures
approximately 63" from beginning ch, ending by
working Row 6.
Finish off.

Holding 6 strands of yarn together, each 20" long,
add fringe in each space across short edges of
Afghan (*Figs. 22a & c, page 142*).

SUNRISE RIPPLE

The first pale rays of the rising sun streak the morning sky, promising a perfect summer day. Cluster stitches come together to create the movement of sunlight across this heavenly blue afghan.

Finished Size: 46" x 63"

MATERIALS

Worsted Weight Yarn:
   Blue - 22 ounces, (620 grams, 1,445 yards)
   Yellow - 10 ounces, (280 grams, 655 yards)
   Dk Blue - 9 ounces, (260 grams, 590 yards)
Crochet hook, size H (5.00 mm) **or** size needed
   for gauge

GAUGE: One repeat from point to point = $3^1/_2$ "
         and 6 rows = 4"

Gauge Swatch: 7"w x 4"h
Ch 35 **loosely**.
Work same as Afghan for 6 rows.
Finish off.

STITCH GUIDE

BEGINNING CLUSTER (uses first 3 sts)
Ch 2, turn; ★ YO, insert hook in **next** st, YO and pull up a loop, YO and draw through 2 loops on hook; repeat from ★ once **more**, YO and draw through all 3 loops on hook *(Figs. 12a & b, page 139)*.
CLUSTER (uses next 5 sts)
YO, insert hook in **next** st, YO and pull up a loop, YO and draw through 2 loops on hook, ★ YO, skip **next** ch, insert hook in **next** st, YO and pull up a loop, YO and draw through 2 loops on hook; repeat from ★ once **more**, YO and draw through all 4 loops on hook *(Figs. 12a & b, page 139)*.
ENDING CLUSTER (uses last 3 sts)
★ YO, insert hook in **next** st, YO and pull up a loop, YO and draw through 2 loops on hook; repeat from ★ 2 times **more**, YO and draw through all 4 loops on hook *(Figs. 12a & b, page 139)*.

COLOR SEQUENCE

2 Rows **each**: Blue, Yellow, Blue, ★ Dk Blue, Blue, Yellow, Blue; repeat from ★ throughout *(Fig. 17a, page 141)*.

AFGHAN

With Blue, ch 211 **loosely**.

Row 1 (Right side): YO, insert hook in fourth ch from hook, YO and pull up a loop, YO and draw through 2 loops on hook, YO, insert hook in next ch, YO and pull up a loop, YO and draw through 2 loops on hook, YO and draw through all 3 loops on hook, ch 1, skip next 2 chs, 5 dc in next ch, ch 1, skip next 2 chs, 7 dc in next ch, ch 1, skip next 2 chs, 5 dc in next ch, ch 1, ★ skip next 2 chs, work Cluster, ch 1, skip next 2 chs, 5 dc in next ch, ch 1, skip next 2 chs, 7 dc in next ch, ch 1, skip next 2 chs, 5 dc in next ch, ch 1; repeat from ★ across to last 5 chs, skip next 2 chs, work ending Cluster: 235 sts and 52 ch-1 sps.

Row 2: Working in Back Loops Only *(Fig. 14, page 140)*, work beginning Cluster, ch 1, skip next 4 dc, 5 dc in next ch, ch 1, skip next 3 dc, 7 dc in next dc, ch 1, skip next 3 dc, 5 dc in next ch, ch 1, ★ skip next 4 dc, work Cluster, ch 1, skip next 4 dc, 5 dc in next ch, ch 1, skip next 3 dc, 7 dc in next dc, ch 1, skip next 3 dc, 5 dc in next ch, ch 1; repeat from ★ across to last 7 sts, skip next 4 dc, work ending Cluster.

Repeat Row 2 until Afghan measures approximately 63" from beginning ch, ending by working 2 rows Blue.

Finish off.

PATRIOTIC STARBURST

Like the spectacular fireworks that fill the sky on Independence Day, this stunning throw will lift your patriotic spirit! Stitch the two styles of squares first, then follow the placement diagram for easy assembly.

Finished Size: 56" x 62"

MATERIALS
Worsted Weight Yarn:
Blue - 54 ounces, (1,530 grams, 3,055 yards)
Burgundy - 10 ounces, (280 grams, 565 yards)
Ecru - 8 ounces, (230 grams, 455 yards)
Crochet hook, size I (5.50 mm) **or** size needed for gauge
Yarn needle

GAUGE: Each Square = 5^1/$_2$ "

Gauge Swatch: 5^1/$_2$ " square
Work same as Square A.

STITCH GUIDE

POPCORN
Work 4 dc in sp indicated, drop loop from hook, insert hook in first dc of 4-dc group, hook dropped loop and pull through.

SQUARE A (Make 74)
With Ecru, ch 4; join with slip st to form a ring.
Rnd 1 (Right side): Ch 7 **(counts as first tr plus ch 3)**, (tr in ring, ch 3) 7 times; join with slip st to first tr changing to Burgundy *(Fig. 17a, page 141)*: 8 tr and 8 ch-3 sps.
Note: Mark Rnd 1 as **right** side.
Rnd 2: Ch 4 **(counts as first hdc plus ch 2)**, work Popcorn in next ch-3 sp, ch 2, ★ hdc in next tr, ch 2, work Popcorn in next ch-3 sp, ch 2; repeat from ★ around; join with slip st to first hdc changing to Blue: 8 Popcorns and 16 ch-2 sps.
Rnd 3: Ch 1, sc in same st and in next ch-2 sp, ch 2, skip next Popcorn, (3 dc, ch 3, 3 dc) in next hdc, ch 2, skip next Popcorn, ★ sc in next ch-2 sp, sc in next hdc and in next ch-2 sp, ch 2, skip next Popcorn, (3 dc, ch 3, 3 dc) in next hdc, ch 2, skip next Popcorn; repeat from ★ 2 times **more**, sc in last ch-2 sp; join with slip st to first sc: 36 sts and 12 sps.

Rnd 4: Slip st in next sc and next ch-2 sp, ch 3 **(counts as first dc, now and throughout)**, 2 dc in same sp, ch 1, (3 dc, ch 3, 3 dc) in next ch-3 sp, ch 1, ★ (3 dc in next ch-2 sp, ch 1) twice, (3 dc, ch 3, 3 dc) in next ch-3 sp, ch 1; repeat from ★ 2 times **more**, 3 dc in last ch-2 sp, ch 1; join with slip st to first dc: 48 dc and 16 sps.
Rnd 5: Slip st in next 2 dc and in next ch-1 sp, ch 3, 2 dc in same sp, ch 1, (3 dc, ch 3, 3 dc) in next ch-3 sp, ch 1, ★ (3 dc in next ch-1 sp, ch 1) 3 times, (3 dc, ch 3, 3 dc) in next ch-3 sp, ch 1; repeat from ★ 2 times **more**, (3 dc in next ch-1 sp, ch 1) twice; join with slip st to first dc, finish off: 60 dc and 20 sps.

SQUARE B (Make 36)
With Burgundy, ch 4; join with slip st to form a ring.
Rnd 1 (Right side): Ch 7, (tr in ring, ch 3) 7 times; join with slip st to first tr changing to Ecru: 8 tr and 8 ch-3 sps.
Note: Mark Rnd 1 as **right** side.
Rnds 2-5: Work same as Square A.

ASSEMBLY
With Blue, using Placement Diagram as a guide and working through **inside** loops only, whipstitch Squares together forming 10 vertical strips of 11 Squares each *(Fig. 20a, page 142)*, beginning in center ch of first corner and ending in center ch of next corner; then whipstitch strips together in same manner.

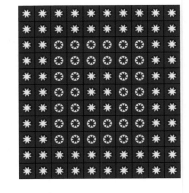

PLACEMENT DIAGRAM

KEY

✳ - A

✺ - B

Continued on page 48.

EDGING

With **right** side facing, join Blue with slip st in any corner ch-3 sp; ch 3, (2 dc, ch 3, 3 dc) in same sp, ch 1, (3 dc in next sp, ch 1) across to next corner ch-3 sp, ★ (3 dc, ch 3, 3 dc) in corner ch-3 sp, ch 1, (3 dc in next sp, ch 1) across to next corner ch-3 sp; repeat from ★ 2 times **more**; join with slip st to first dc, finish off.

FINISHING

Holding 8 strands of Blue together, add fringe in each sp across short edges of Afghan *(Figs. 22a & c, page 142)*.

SUMMER LACE

With its unique and airy pattern, this intricate wrap would make a lovely offering for a summer bride. Worked in strips using brushed acrylic yarn, it's sure to become an heirloom.

Finished Size: 48" x 63"

MATERIALS

Worsted Weight Brushed Acrylic Yarn:
   32 ounces, (910 grams, 2,470 yards)
Crochet hook, size H (5.00 mm) **or** size needed
   for gauge

GAUGE: Each Strip = 5$\frac{1}{4}$" wide

STITCH GUIDE

> **SMALL PICOT**
> Ch 2, slip st in second ch from hook.
> **LARGE PICOT**
> Ch 3, slip st in third ch from hook.

STRIP (Make 9)

Ch 21.
Row 1 (Right side): (3 Dc, ch 2, 3 dc) in fifth ch from hook, skip next 3 chs, slip st in next ch, ch 3, skip next 3 chs, (sc, ch 6, sc) in next ch, ch 3, skip next 3 chs, slip st in next ch, skip next 3 chs, (3 dc, ch 2, 3 dc) in last ch: 5 sps and one loop.
Note: Mark Row 2 as **right** side and bottom edge.
Row 2: Ch 5, turn; (3 dc, ch 2, 3 dc) in first ch-2 sp, skip next ch-3 sp, [tr, (work small Picot, dc) 3 times] in next loop, work 3 large Picots, slip st in base of first large Picot, [(dc, work small Picot) 3 times, tr] in same loop, skip next ch-3 sp, (3 dc, ch 2, 3 dc) in last ch-2 sp: 9 Picots and 2 ch-2 sps.

Row 3: Ch 5, turn; (3 dc, ch 2, 3 dc) in first ch-2 sp, skip next 2 small Picots, slip st in next small Picot, ch 5, skip next large Picot, slip st in next large Picot, ch 5, skip next large Picot, slip st in next small Picot, (3 dc, ch 2, 3 dc) in last ch-2 sp: 2 sps and 3 loops.
Row 4: Ch 5, turn; (3 dc, ch 2, 3 dc) in first ch-2 sp, ch 3, skip next loop, sc in next slip st, ch 3, skip next loop, (3 dc, ch 2, 3 dc) in last ch-2 sp: 4 sps and one loop.
Row 5: Ch 5, turn; (3 dc, ch 2, 3 dc) in first ch-2 sp, ch 3, (sc, ch 6, sc) in next sc, ch 3, skip next ch-3 sp, (3 dc, ch 2, 3 dc) in last ch-2 sp: 4 sps and 2 loops.
Repeat Rows 2-5 until Strip measures approximately 63" from beginning ch, ending by working Row 3. Finish off.

JOINING

Holding two Strips with **right** sides together, having markers at same end and starting at bottom, join yarn with slip st in first loop on **back Strip** in end of Row 1; ch 3, sc in first loop on **front Strip** *(Fig. 19, page 141)*, ch 3, sc in next loop on **back Strip**, ch 3, ★ sc in next loop on **front Strip**, ch 3, sc in next loop on **back Strip**, ch 3; repeat from ★ across, slip st in last dc on **front Strip**; finish off.
Join remaining Strips in same manner.

OCEAN BEAUTY

You'll have a "whale" of a good time stitching this ocean beauty! Various hues of blue and green give our afghan its eye-catching appearance.

Finished Size: 52" x 70"

MATERIALS
Worsted Weight Yarn:
    White - 9 ounces, (260 grams, 605 yards)
    Aqua - 8 ounces, (230 grams, 540 yards)
    Lt Blue - 5 ounces, (140 grams, 335 yards)
    Teal - 17 ounces, (480 grams, 1,145 yards)
    Turquoise - 8 ounces, (230 grams, 540 yards)
    Dk Blue - 8 ounces, (230 grams, 540 yards)
    Blue - 6 ounces, (170 grams, 405 yards)
    Lt Green - 5 ounces, (140 grams, 335 yards)
Crochet hook, size H (5.00 mm) **or** size needed
    for gauge
Tissue paper
Straight pins
Sewing needle and thread

GAUGE: In pattern, (Shell, sc) twice = $3^1/2$"
        and 8 rows = $4^1/2$"
        14 sc and 16 rows = 4"

STITCH GUIDE

> **SHELL**
> 5 Tr in next sc.

COLOR SEQUENCE
Note: **When changing colors (Fig. 17a, page 141), cut old yarn and work over both ends.**
★ † 3 Rows White, 1 row **each** of Aqua, White, Lt Blue, Teal, Turquoise, Dk Blue, Blue, Lt Green, Teal, Dk Blue, Turquoise, Teal, Blue, Turquoise, Teal, Aqua, Dk Blue, Teal, Lt Blue, Lt Green, Turquoise, Teal, Blue, White, Aqua, 3 rows White †, 2 rows Lt Green, 4 rows Aqua, 2 rows Lt Blue, 2 rows Blue, 1 row Turquoise, 4 rows Dk Blue, 12 rows Teal, 4 rows Dk Blue, 1 row Turquoise, 2 rows Blue, 2 rows Lt Blue, 4 rows Aqua, 2 rows Lt Green; repeat from ★ once **more**, then repeat from † to † once.

AFGHAN BODY
With White, ch 183 **loosely**.
Row 1: Dc in fourth ch from hook and in each ch across: 181 sts.
Row 2 (Right side): Ch 3 **(counts as first dc, now and throughout)**, turn; dc in next dc and in each st across.
Note: Mark Row 2 as **right** side and bottom edge.
Row 3: Ch 1, turn; sc in first 2 dc, hdc in next dc, dc in next dc, hdc in next dc, ★ sc in next 3 dc, hdc in next dc, dc in next dc, hdc in next dc; repeat from ★ across to last 2 dc, sc in last 2 dc.
Row 4: Ch 4 **(counts as first tr, now and throughout)**, turn; 2 tr in same st, skip next 2 sts, sc in next dc, ★ skip next 2 sts, work Shell, skip next 2 sts, sc in next dc; repeat from ★ across to last 3 sts, skip next 2 sts, 3 tr in last sc: 29 Shells.
Row 5: Ch 1, turn; sc in first tr, work Shell, ★ sc in center tr of next Shell, work Shell; repeat from ★ across to last 3 tr, skip next 2 tr, sc in last tr: 30 Shells.
Row 6: Ch 4, turn; 2 tr in same st, sc in center tr of next Shell, ★ work Shell, sc in center tr of next Shell; repeat from ★ across to last sc, 3 tr in last sc: 29 Shells.
Rows 7-28: Repeat Rows 5 and 6, 11 times.
Row 29: Ch 1, turn; sc in first 2 tr, hdc in next tr, dc in next sc, hdc in next tr, ★ sc in next 3 tr, hdc in next tr, dc in next sc, hdc in next tr; repeat from ★ across to last 2 tr, sc in last 2 tr: 181 sts.
Rows 30 and 31: Ch 3, turn; dc in next st and in each st across.
Rows 32-73: Ch 1, turn; sc in each st across.
Rows 74 and 75: Ch 3, turn; dc in next st and in each st across.
Rows 76-177: Repeat Rows 3-75 once; then repeat Rows 3-31 once **more**.
Finish off.

Continued on page 52.

WHALES

On tissue paper, trace 5 Whale patterns. Cut out each pattern along dotted line.

Using photo as a guide for placement:
With **right** side of Afghan facing and bottom edge toward you, arrange 5 Whales facing in the same direction between Rows 47 and 58; pin in place.
With sewing needle and thread, baste along the outline of each Whale. Tear away tissue paper.
With **right** side of Afghan facing, using Turquoise and holding yarn at back of Afghan, insert hook from **front** to **back** at center of Whale's tail, YO and pull up a loop; working along the thread outline, ★ insert hook in next stitch/row, YO and draw **loosely** through loop on hook; repeat from ★ around entire thread outline; finish off.
Remove thread outline.
Repeat for remaining 4 Whales.

With top edge toward you, repeat for remaining 5 Whales between Rows 120 and 131.

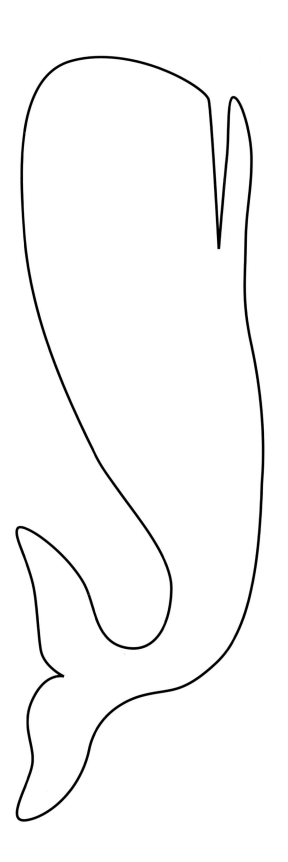

52

LADYBUGS

The young-at-heart will be charmed by this whimsical wrap! Diamond and ladybug squares alternate to create the bright and happy design.

Finished Size: 32$\frac{1}{2}$" x 44$\frac{1}{2}$"

MATERIALS
Sport Weight Yarn:
    White - 17$\frac{1}{2}$ ounces, (500 grams, 1,750 yards)
    Red - 4 ounces, (110 grams, 400 yards)
    Black - 1 ounce, (30 grams, 100 yards)
Crochet hook, size G (4.00 mm) **or** size needed
    for gauge
Yarn needle

GAUGE: 15 sc and 17 rows = 4$\frac{1}{4}$ "
              Each Square = 6"

Gauge Swatch: 4$\frac{1}{4}$ " square
Work same as Diamond Square through Row 17.

STITCH GUIDE

CLUSTER (uses one sc)
★ YO, insert hook in Back Loop Only of sc indicated *(Fig. 14, page 140)*, YO and pull up a loop, YO and draw through 2 loops on hook; repeat from ★ 3 times **more**, YO and draw through all 5 loops on hook *(Figs. 11a & b, page 139)*.
SCALLOP
(Slip st, ch 2, dc) in sp indicated.

DIAMOND SQUARE (Make 17)
With White, ch 16 **loosely**.
Row 1: Sc in second ch from hook and in each ch across: 15 sc.
Row 2 (Right side): Ch 1, turn; sc in each sc across.
Note: Mark Row 2 as **right** side and bottom edge.
Rows 3 and 4: Ch 1, turn; sc in each sc across.
Work in **both** loops of each stitch unless otherwise indicated.
Row 5: Ch 1, turn; sc in first 7 sc, work Cluster in next sc, sc in last 7 sc: 14 sc and one Cluster.
Row 6: Ch 1, turn; sc in each st across: 15 sc.
Row 7: Ch 1, turn; sc in first 5 sc, work Cluster in next sc, sc in next 3 sc, work Cluster in next sc, sc in last 5 sc: 13 sc and 2 Clusters.

Row 8: Ch 1, turn; sc in each st across: 15 sc.
Row 9: Ch 1, turn; sc in first 3 sc, work Cluster in next sc, sc in next 7 sc, work Cluster in next sc, sc in last 3 sc: 13 sc and 2 Clusters.
Row 10: Ch 1, turn; sc in each st across: 15 sc.
Row 11: Ch 1, turn; sc in first 5 sc, work Cluster in next sc, sc in next 3 sc, work Cluster in next sc, sc in last 5 sc: 13 sc and 2 Clusters.
Row 12: Ch 1, turn; sc in each st across: 15 sc.
Row 13: Ch 1, turn; sc in first 7 sc, work Cluster in next sc, sc in last 7 sc: 14 sc and one Cluster.
Rows 14-17: Ch 1, turn; sc in each st across; do **not** finish off.

BORDER
Rnd 1: Ch 1, turn; sc in each sc across, † ch 3; working in end of rows, sc in first 5 rows, (skip next row, sc in next 5 rows) twice, ch 3 †; working in free loops of beginning ch *(Fig. 15b, page 140)*, sc in ch at base of first sc and in each ch across, repeat from † to † once; join with slip st to first sc, finish off: 60 sc and 4 ch-3 sps.
Rnd 2: With **right** side facing, join Red with sc in sc before any corner ch-3 sp *(see Joining With Sc, page 140)*; ★ † (sc, ch 3, sc) in next corner ch-3 sp, sc in next sc, ch 1, skip next sc, (sc in next 2 sc, ch 1, skip next sc) 4 times †, sc in next sc; repeat from ★ 2 times **more**, then repeat from † to † once; join with slip st to first sc, finish off: 48 sc and 24 sps.
Rnd 3: With **right** side facing, join White with slip st in any corner ch-3 sp; ch 3 **(counts as first dc, now and throughout)**, (dc, ch 3, 2 dc) in same sp, ch 1, ★ (2 dc in next ch-1 sp, ch 1) across to next corner ch-3 sp, (2 dc, ch 3, 2 dc) in corner ch-3 sp, ch 1; repeat from ★ 2 times **more**, (2 dc in next ch-1 sp, ch 1) across; join with slip st to first dc, finish off: 56 dc and 28 sps.

Continued on page 54.

LADYBUG SQUARE (Make 18)

With White, ch 16 **loosely**.

Row 1: Sc in second ch from hook and in each ch across: 15 sc.

Row 2 (Right side): Ch 1, turn; sc in each sc across.

Note: Mark Row 2 as **right** side and bottom edge. When changing colors *(Fig. 17a, page 141)*, do **not** carry yarn across back of work. Use a separate ball of yarn for each color change. Cut yarn when color is no longer needed.

Row 3: Ch 1, turn; sc in first 5 sc changing to Red in last sc, sc in next 2 sc changing to Black in last sc, sc in next sc changing to Red, sc in next 2 sc changing to White in last sc, sc in last 5 sc.

Continue to change colors in same manner throughout.

Row 4: Ch 1, turn; sc in first 4 sc, with Red sc in next 3 sc, with Black sc in next sc, with Red sc in next 3 sc, with White sc in last 4 sc.

Rows 5-11: Ch 1, turn; sc in first 3 sc, with Red sc in next 4 sc, with Black sc in next sc, with Red sc in next 4 sc, with White sc in last 3 sc.

Row 12: Ch 1, turn; sc in first 4 sc, with Red sc in next 3 sc, with Black sc in next sc, with Red sc in next 3 sc, with White sc in last 4 sc.

Rows 13 and 14: Ch 1, turn; sc in first 5 sc, with Black sc in next 5 sc, with White sc in last 5 sc.

Row 15: Ch 1, turn; sc in first 6 sc, with Black sc in next 3 sc, with White sc in last 6 sc.

Rows 16 and 17: Ch 1, turn; sc in each sc across; do **not** finish off.

Work Border, page 53.

Spot (Make 2): With Black and leaving a 6" length for sewing, ch 2, YO, insert hook in second ch from hook, YO and pull up a loop, YO and draw through 2 loops on hook, YO, insert hook in same ch, YO and pull up a loop, YO and draw through 2 loops on hook, YO and draw through all 3 loops on hook, ch 1; finish off.

Using photo as a guide, sew Spots to Ladybug.

ASSEMBLY

With White, hold bottom edge of one Square to top edge of next Square. Using Placement Diagram as a guide and working through **both** loops, whipstitch Squares together forming 5 vertical strips of 7 Squares each *(Fig. 20b, page 142)*; then whipstitch strips together, keeping bottom edges at same end.

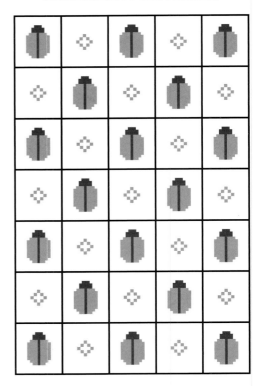

EDGING

Rnd 1: With **right** side facing, join White with slip st in any corner ch-3 sp; ch 3, (dc, ch 3, 2 dc) in same sp, ch 1, ★ (2 dc in next sp, ch 1) across to next corner ch-3 sp, (2 dc, ch 3, 2 dc) in corner ch-3 sp, ch 1; repeat from ★ 2 times **more**, (2 dc in next sp, ch 1) across; join with slip st to first dc: 384 dc and 192 sps.

Rnd 2: Slip st in next dc and in next corner ch-3 sp, ch 3, (dc, ch 3, 2 dc) in same sp, ch 1, ★ (2 dc in next ch-1 sp, ch 1) across to next corner ch-3 sp, (2 dc, ch 3, 2 dc) in corner ch-3 sp, ch 1; repeat from ★ 2 times **more**, (2 dc in next ch-1 sp, ch 1) across; join with slip st to first dc: 392 dc and 196 sps.

Rnd 3: Slip st in next dc, work (Scallop, ch 2, Scallop) in next corner ch-3 sp, ★ work Scallop in each ch-1 sp across to next corner ch-3 sp, work (Scallop, ch 2, Scallop) in corner ch-3 sp; repeat from ★ 2 times **more**, work Scallop in each ch-1 sp across; join with slip st to slip st at base of first Scallop, finish off.

LOVELY LOOK

Remember those wonderful chenille bedspreads our mothers and grandmothers used? This diamond-studded wrap captures that same lovely look and soft feel using long double crochet stitches.

Finished Size: 53^1/$_2$" x 67"

MATERIALS
Worsted Weight Yarn:
62 ounces, (1,760 grams, 4,250 yards)
Crochet hook, size I (5.50 mm) **or** size needed for gauge

GAUGE: 15 sc and 14 rows = 4"

Gauge Swatch: 4" square
Ch 16 **loosely**.
Row 1 (Right side): Sc in second ch from hook and in each ch across; finish off: 15 sc.
Rows 2-14: With **right** side facing and working in Back Loops Only *(Fig. 14, page 140)*, join yarn with sc in first sc; sc in next sc and in each sc across; finish off.

STITCH GUIDE

LONG DOUBLE CROCHET *(abbreviated LDC)*
Working in **front** of next sc, YO, insert hook in free loop *(Fig. 1)* of st one row **below** next sc, YO and pull up a loop, (YO and draw through 2 loops on hook) twice. Skip sc behind LDC.

Fig. 1

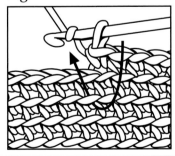

Note: Each row is worked across length of Afghan, with **right** side facing and working in Back Loops Only *(Fig. 14, page 140)*. When joining yarn and finishing off, leave a 6" length for fringe.

AFGHAN BODY
Ch 252 **loosely**.
Row 1 (Right side): Sc in second ch from hook and in each ch across; finish off: 251 sc.
Note: Mark Row 1 as **right** side.
Rows 2 and 3: Join yarn with sc in first sc *(see Joining With Sc, page 140)*; sc in next sc and in each sc across; finish off.
Row 4: Join yarn with sc in first sc; sc in next 4 sc, work LDC, ★ sc in next 19 sts, work LDC; repeat from ★ across to last 5 sc, sc in last 5 sc; finish off: 238 sc and 13 LDC.
Row 5: Join yarn with sc in first sc; sc in next 5 sts, work LDC, sc in next 17 sts, work LDC, ★ sc in next st, work LDC, sc in next 17 sts, work LDC; repeat from ★ across to last 6 sts, sc in last 6 sts; finish off: 227 sc and 24 LDC.
Row 6: Join yarn with sc in first sc; sc in next 6 sts, work LDC, sc in next 15 sts, work LDC, ★ sc in next 3 sts, work LDC, sc in next 15 sts, work LDC; repeat from ★ across to last 7 sts, sc in last 7 sts; finish off.
Row 7: Join yarn with sc in first sc; sc in next 7 sts, work LDC, sc in next 13 sts, work LDC, ★ sc in next 5 sts, work LDC, sc in next 13 sts, work LDC; repeat from ★ across to last 8 sts, sc in last 8 sts; finish off.
Row 8: Join yarn with sc in first sc; sc in next 8 sts, work LDC, sc in next 11 sts, work LDC, ★ (sc in next 3 sts, work LDC) twice, sc in next 11 sts, work LDC; repeat from ★ across to last 9 sts, sc in last 9 sts; finish off: 216 sc and 35 LDC.
Row 9: Join yarn with sc in first sc; (sc in next 9 sts, work LDC) twice, ★ sc in next 3 sts, work LDC, sc in next st, work LDC, sc in next 3 sts, work LDC, sc in next 9 sts, work LDC; repeat from ★ across to last 10 sts, sc in last 10 sts; finish off: 205 sc and 46 LDC.
Row 10: Join yarn with sc in first sc; sc in next 10 sts, work LDC, sc in next 7 sts, work LDC, ★ (sc in next 3 sts, work LDC) 3 times, sc in next 7 sts, work LDC; repeat from ★ across to last 11 sts, sc in last 11 sts; finish off.

Continued on page 58.

Row 11: Join yarn with sc in first sc; sc in next 11 sts, work LDC, sc in next 5 sts, work LDC, ★ sc in next 3 sts, work LDC, sc in next 5 sts, work LDC; repeat from ★ across to last 12 sts, sc in last 12 sts; finish off.

Row 12: Join yarn with sc in first sc; sc in next 12 sts, work LDC, (sc in next 3 sts, work LDC) across to last 13 sts, sc in last 13 sts; finish off: 194 sc and 57 LDC.

Row 13: Join yarn with sc in first sc; sc in next 13 sts, work LDC, sc in next sc, work LDC, ★ (sc in next 3 sts, work LDC) twice, sc in next st, work LDC; repeat from ★ across to last 14 sts, sc in last 14 sts; finish off: 183 sc and 68 LDC.

Row 14: Join yarn with sc in first sc; sc in next 14 sts, work LDC, (sc in next 3 sts, work LDC) across to last 15 sts, sc in last 15 sts; finish off: 195 sc and 56 LDC.

Row 15: Join yarn with sc in first sc; sc in next 13 sc, work LDC, sc in next LDC, work LDC, ★ (sc in next 3 sts, work LDC) twice, sc in next st, work LDC; repeat from ★ across to last 14 sc, sc in last 14 sc; finish off: 183 sc and 68 LDC.

Row 16: Join yarn with sc in first sc; sc in next 12 sc, work LDC, (sc in next 3 sts, work LDC) across to last 13 sc, sc in last 13 sc; finish off: 194 sc and 57 LDC.

Row 17: Join yarn with sc in first sc; sc in next 11 sc, work LDC, sc in next 5 sts, work LDC, ★ sc in next 3 sts, work LDC, sc in next 5 sts, work LDC; repeat from ★ across to last 12 sc, sc in last 12 sc; finish off: 205 sc and 46 LDC.

Row 18: Join yarn with sc in first sc; sc in next 10 sc, work LDC, (sc in next 3 sts, work LDC) across to last 11 sc, sc in last 11 sc; finish off: 193 sc and 58 LDC.

Row 19: Join yarn with sc in first sc; sc in next 9 sc, work LDC, sc in next 3 sts, work LDC, sc in next LDC, work LDC, ★ (sc in next 3 sts, work LDC) twice, sc in next st, work LDC; repeat from ★ across to last 14 sts, sc in next 3 sts, work LDC, sc in last 10 sc; finish off: 181 sc and 70 LDC.

Row 20: Join yarn with sc in first sc; sc in next 8 sc, work LDC, (sc in next 3 sts, work LDC) across to last 9 sc, sc in last 9 sc; finish off: 192 sc and 59 LDC.

Row 21: Join yarn with sc in first sc; sc in next 7 sc, work LDC, sc in next 3 sts, work LDC, ★ sc in next 5 sts, work LDC, sc in next 3 sts, work LDC; repeat from ★ across to last 8 sc, sc in last 8 sc; finish off: 203 sc and 48 LDC.

Row 22: Join yarn with sc in first sc; sc in next 6 sc, work LDC, (sc in next 3 sts, work LDC) across to last 7 sc, sc in last 7 sc; finish off: 191 sc and 60 LDC.

Row 23: Join yarn with sc in first sc; sc in next 5 sc, work LDC, (sc in next 3 sts, work LDC) twice, ★ sc in next st, work LDC, (sc in next 3 sts, work LDC) twice; repeat from ★ across to last 6 sc, sc in last 6 sc; finish off: 179 sc and 72 LDC.

Row 24: Join yarn with sc in first sc; sc in next 4 sc, work LDC, (sc in next 3 sts, work LDC) across to last 5 sc, sc in last 5 sc; finish off: 190 sc and 61 LDC.

Row 25: Join yarn with sc in first sc; sc in next 5 sts, work LDC, (sc in next 3 sts, work LDC) twice, ★ sc in next st, work LDC, (sc in next 3 sts, work LDC) twice; repeat from ★ across to last 6 sts, sc in last 6 sts; finish off: 179 sc and 72 LDC.

Row 26: Join yarn with sc in first sc; sc in next 6 sts, work LDC, (sc in next 3 sts, work LDC) across to last 7 sts, sc in last 7 sts; finish off: 191 sc and 60 LDC.

Row 27: Join yarn with sc in first sc; sc in next 7 sts, work LDC, sc in next 3 sts, work LDC, ★ sc in next 5 sts, work LDC, sc in next 3 sts, work LDC; repeat from ★ across to last 8 sts, sc in last 8 sts; finish off: 203 sc and 48 LDC.

Row 28: Join yarn with sc in first sc; sc in next 8 sts, work LDC, (sc in next 3 sts, work LDC) across to last 9 sts, sc in last 9 sts; finish off: 192 sc and 59 LDC.

Row 29: Join yarn with sc in first sc; sc in next 9 sts, work LDC, sc in next 3 sts, work LDC, sc in next sc, work LDC, ★ (sc in next 3 sts, work LDC) twice, sc in next st, work LDC; repeat from ★ across to last 14 sts, sc in next 3 sts, work LDC, sc in last 10 sts; finish off: 181 sc and 70 LDC.

Row 30: Join yarn with sc in first sc; sc in next 10 sts, work LDC, (sc in next 3 sts, work LDC) across to last 11 sts, sc in last 11 sts; finish off: 193 sc and 58 LDC.

Rows 31-177: Repeat Rows 11-30, 7 times; then repeat Rows 11-17 once **more**.

Row 178: Repeat Row 10.
Row 179: Repeat Row 9.
Row 180: Repeat Row 8.
Row 181: Repeat Row 7.
Row 182: Repeat Row 6.
Row 183: Repeat Row 5.
Row 184: Repeat Row 4.
Rows 185-187: Join yarn with sc in first sc; sc in next st and in each st across; finish off.

TRIM

With **right** side facing and working in free loops of beginning ch *(Fig. 15b, page 140)*, join yarn with sc in first ch; sc in next 250 chs; finish off.

Holding 2 strands of yarn together, each 13" long, add additional fringe to end of every other row across short edges of Afghan *(Figs. 22b & d, page 142)*.

ROSEBUD

Reminiscent of days gone by, the large blocks on this afghan display charming quilt-like designs. The same block stitches used to create the folk-art florals also form the sweet rosebud border.

Finished Size: 41" x 57"

MATERIALS

Worsted Weight Yarn:
    Ecru - 26 ounces, (740 grams, 1,470 yards)
    Rose - 12 ounces, (340 grams, 680 yards)
    Green - $6^1/_2$ ounces, (180 grams, 370 yards)
    Pink - 2 ounces, (60 grams, 115 yards)
Crochet hook, size H (5.00 mm) **or** size needed
    for gauge
Yarn needle

GAUGE: Each Small Square = $7^3/_4$ ";
            Each Large Square = 17"

Gauge Swatch: $5^3/_4$ " x $5^3/_4$ " x $8^1/_4$ "
Work same as Small Square for 7 rows.

STITCH GUIDE

BEGINNING BLOCK
Ch 6 **loosely**, turn; dc in fourth ch from hook and in next 2 chs.
BLOCK
Slip st in ch-3 sp of next Block, ch 3, 3 dc in same sp.

SYMBOL CROCHET CHART

KEY

◯ - chain

⬬ - slip st

╤ -double crochet

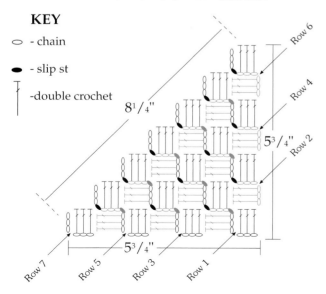

SMALL SQUARE (Make 24)

Row 1 (Right side): With Rose, ch 6 **loosely**, dc in fourth ch from hook and in next 2 chs changing to Green in last dc *(Fig. 17a, page 141)*: one Block.
Note: Mark Row 1 as **right** side.
Row 2: Work Beginning Block, slip st around beginning ch of previous Block *(Fig. 1)*, ch 3, 3 dc in same sp changing to Ecru in last dc *(Fig. 2)*: 2 Blocks.

Fig. 1

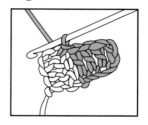

Fig. 2

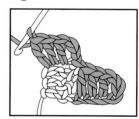

Note: Continue to change colors in same manner.
Row 3: Work Beginning Block, slip st in ch-3 sp of first Block, ch 3, 3 dc in same sp, work Block: 3 Blocks.
Row 4: Work Beginning Block, slip st in ch-3 sp of first Block, ch 3, 3 dc in same sp, with Green, work Block, with Ecru, work Block: 4 Blocks.
Row 5: Work Beginning Block, slip st in ch-3 sp of first Block, ch 3, 3 dc in same sp, work Block, with Green, work Block, with Ecru, work Block: 5 Blocks.
Row 6: Work Beginning Block, with Pink, slip st in ch-3 sp of first Block, ch 3, 3 dc in same sp, with Green, work 2 Blocks, with Ecru, work 2 Blocks: 6 Blocks.
Row 7: Work Beginning Block, slip st in ch-3 sp of first Block, ch 3, 3 dc in same sp, work 2 Blocks, with Green, work Block, with Ecru, work 2 Blocks: 7 Blocks.
Row 8: Work Beginning Block, slip st in ch-3 sp of first Block, ch 3, 3 dc in same sp, work 2 Blocks, ★ with Green, work Block, with Ecru, work Block; repeat from ★ once **more**: 8 Blocks.

Continued on page 60.

Row 9: Work Beginning Block, with Pink, slip st in ch-3 sp of first Block, ch 3, 3 dc in same sp, with Green, work 2 Blocks, with Ecru, work 5 Blocks; do **not** finish off: 9 Blocks.

Row 10: Work Beginning Block, slip st in ch-3 sp of first Block, ch 3, 3 dc in same sp, work Block, with Rose, work 2 Blocks, with Ecru, work 2 Blocks, with Green, work Block, with Ecru, work 2 Blocks: 10 Blocks.

Row 11: Turn; slip st in first 3 dc and in next ch-3 sp, ch 3, 3 dc in same sp, work 2 Blocks, with Green, work Block, with Rose, work 3 Blocks, with Ecru, work 2 Blocks, slip st in ch-3 sp of last Block: 9 Blocks.

Row 12: Turn; slip st in first 3 dc and in next ch-3 sp, ch 3, 3 dc in same sp, work Block, with Rose, work 3 Blocks, with Ecru, work 3 Blocks, slip st in ch-3 sp of last Block: 8 Blocks.

Row 13: Turn; slip st in first 3 dc and in next ch-3 sp, ch 3, 3 dc in same sp, work 2 Blocks, with Rose, work Block, with Pink, work Block, with Rose, work Block, with Ecru, work Block, slip st in ch-3 sp of last Block: 7 Blocks.

Row 14: Turn; slip st in first 3 dc and in next ch-3 sp, ch 3, 3 dc in same sp, with Rose, work 3 Blocks, with Ecru, work 2 Blocks, slip st in ch-3 sp of last Block: 6 Blocks.

Row 15: Turn; slip st in first 3 dc and in next ch-3 sp, ch 3, 3 dc in same sp, work Block, with Rose, work 2 Blocks, with Ecru, work Block, slip st in ch-3 sp of last Block: 5 Blocks.

Row 16: Turn; slip st in first 3 dc and in next ch-3 sp, ch 3, 3 dc in same sp, work 3 Blocks, slip st in ch-3 sp of last Block: 4 Blocks.

Row 17: Turn; slip st in first 3 dc and in next ch-3 sp, ch 3, 3 dc in same sp, work 2 Blocks, slip st in ch-3 sp of last Block: 3 Blocks.

Row 18: Turn; slip st in first 3 dc and in next ch-3 sp, ch 3, 3 dc in same sp, work Block, slip st in ch-3 sp of last Block: 2 Blocks.

Row 19: Turn; slip st in first 3 dc and in next ch-3 sp, ch 3, 3 dc in same sp, slip st in ch-3 sp of last Block; finish off: one Block.

LARGE SQUARE (Make 6)

Holding Small Squares with **wrong** sides together, Row 1 in center, and matching colors as needed, sew 4 Small Squares together to form one Large Square.

BORDER

Rnd 1: With **right** side facing, join Ecru with sc in top of ch-3 in any corner (Row 19) *(see Joining With Sc, page 140)*; ch 2, sc in same st, ch 2, ★ † skip next 3 sts, sc in next st, ch 2, skip next 2 chs, (sc in next st, ch 2, skip next 3 sts, sc in next st, ch 2, skip next 2 chs) 9 times †, (sc, ch 2) twice in next ch; repeat from ★ 2 times **more**, then repeat from † to † once; join with slip st to first sc, finish off: 84 ch-2 sps.

Rnd 2: With **right** side facing, join Rose with slip st in any corner ch-2 sp; ch 3, (dc, ch 2, 2 dc) in same sp, 3 dc in each ch-2 sp across to next corner ch-2 sp, ★ (2 dc, ch 2, 2 dc) in corner ch-2 sp, 3 dc in each ch-2 sp across to next corner ch-2 sp; repeat from ★ 2 times **more**; join with slip st to top of beginning ch-3, finish off: 256 dc and 4 ch-2 sps.

ASSEMBLY

With Rose and working through **inside** loops, whipstitch Large Squares together forming 2 vertical strips of 3 Large Squares each *(Fig. 20a, page 142)*, beginning in second ch of first corner ch-2 and ending in first ch of next corner ch-2; then whipstitch strips together in same manner.

EDGING

Rnd 1: With **right** side facing and working in Back Loops Only *(Fig. 14, page 140)*, join Rose with sc in first ch of upper right corner ch-2; ch 2, sc in next ch, † work 125 sc evenly spaced across to next corner ch-2, sc in next ch, ch 2, sc in next ch, work 185 sc evenly spaced across to next corner ch-2 †, sc in next ch, ch 2, sc in next ch, repeat from † to † once; join with slip st to first sc, finish off: 628 sc.

Rnd 2: With **right** side facing, join Green with sc in upper right corner ch-2 sp; (slip st, ch 3, 3 dc) in same sp, skip next 3 sc, (slip st, ch 3, 3 dc) in next sc, ★ † with Ecru, skip next 3 sc, (slip st, ch 3, 3 dc) in next sc, with Green, [skip next 3 sc, (slip st, ch 3, 3 dc) in next sc] twice †, repeat from † to † across to within 3 sc of next corner ch-2 sp, skip next 3 sc, (sc, slip st, ch 3, 3 dc) in corner ch-2 sp, skip next 3 sc, (slip st, ch 3, 3 dc) in next sc; repeat from ★ 2 times **more**, then repeat from † to † across to last 3 sc, skip last 3 sc; join with slip st to first sc changing to Ecru: 158 Blocks and 4 sc.

Rnd 3: Ch 3, **turn**; 3 dc in same st, with Pink, work Block, ★ † (with Ecru, work 2 Blocks, with Pink, work Block) across to within one Block of next corner sc, with Ecru, work Block †, (slip st, ch 3, 3 dc) in corner sc, with Pink, work Block; repeat from ★ 2 times **more**, then repeat from † to † once; join with slip st in sc at base of beginning ch-3: 162 Blocks.

Rnd 4: Turn; (slip st, ch 3, 3 dc) in first dc, † (slip st, ch 3, 3 dc) in ch-3 sp of same Block, work 32 Blocks, (slip st, ch 3, 3 dc) in first dc of next Block, (slip st, ch 3, 3 dc) in ch-3 sp of same Block, work 47 Blocks †, (slip st, ch 3, 3 dc) in first dc of next Block, repeat from † to † once; join with slip st in same st as first slip st changing to Rose: 166 Blocks.

Rnd 5: Turn; (slip st, ch 3, 3 dc) in first dc, † (slip st, ch 3, 3 dc) in ch-3 sp of same Block, work 47 Blocks, (slip st, ch 3, 3 dc) in first dc of next Block, (slip st, ch 3, 3 dc) in ch-3 sp of same Block, work 33 Blocks †, (slip st, ch 3, 3 dc) in first dc of next Block, repeat from † to † once; join with slip st in same st as first slip st, finish off.

DIAMOND RIPPLE

*Wrap yourself in the rich warmth of this cozy summer afghan. Worked in rows,
our elegant throw is the perfect partner for curling up with a good book.*

Finished Size: 53" x 72"

MATERIALS

Worsted Weight Yarn:
57 ounces, (1,620 grams, 3,225 yards)
Crochet hook, size I (5.50 mm) **or** size needed
for gauge

GAUGE: In pattern, from point to point = 3³/₄ ";
8 rows = 6"

Gauge Swatch: 7¹/₂ "w x 6"h
Ch 41 **loosely**.
Work same as Afghan Body for 8 rows.
Finish off.

STITCH GUIDE

DECREASE (uses next 5 sts)
YO, † insert hook in **next** st, YO and pull up a
loop, YO and draw through 2 loops on hook †,
YO, skip next 3 sts, repeat from † to † once, YO
and draw through all 3 loops on hook **(counts as
one dc)**.

AFGHAN BODY

Ch 293 **loosely**.

Row 1: 2 Dc in fourth ch from hook **(3 skipped chs
count as first dc)**, ch 1, skip next ch, (dc in next ch,
ch 1, skip next ch) twice, decrease, ch 1, (skip next
ch, dc in next ch, ch 1) twice, ★ skip next ch, dc in
next 3 chs, ch 3, dc in next 3 chs, ch 1, skip next ch,
(dc in next ch, ch 1, skip next ch) twice, decrease,
ch 1, (skip next ch, dc in next ch, ch 1) twice; repeat
from ★ across to last 2 chs, skip next ch, (2 dc, tr) in
last ch: 153 dc and one tr.

Row 2 (Right side): Ch 3 **(counts as first dc, now
and throughout)**, turn; 2 dc in same st, dc in next
2 dc, ch 1, dc in next dc, ch 1, skip next ch, decrease,
ch 1, dc in next dc, ch 1, ★ dc in next 3 dc, (2 dc,
ch 3, 2 dc) in next ch-3 sp, dc in next 3 dc, ch 1, dc in
next dc, ch 1, skip next ch, decrease, ch 1, dc in next
dc, ch 1; repeat from ★ across to last 3 dc, dc in next
2 dc, (2 dc, tr) in last dc: 181 dc.

Note: Mark Row 2 as **right** side.

Row 3: Ch 3, turn; 2 dc in same st, dc in next 4 dc,
ch 1, skip next ch, decrease, ch 1, ★ dc in next 5 dc,
(2 dc, ch 3, 2 dc) in next ch-3 sp, dc in next 5 dc, ch 1,
skip next ch, decrease, ch 1; repeat from ★ across to
last 5 dc, dc in next 4 dc, (2 dc, tr) in last dc: 209 dc.

Row 4: Ch 3, turn; 2 dc in same st, dc in next 5 dc,
decrease, ★ dc in next 6 dc, (2 dc, ch 3, 2 dc) in next
ch-3 sp, dc in next 6 dc, decrease; repeat from ★
across to last 6 dc, dc in next 5 dc, (2 dc, tr) in last
dc: 237 dc.

Row 5: Ch 3, turn; 2 dc in same st, ch 1, skip next dc,
(dc in next dc, ch 1, skip next dc) twice, decrease,
★ (ch 1, skip next dc, dc in next dc) 3 times, (2 dc,
ch 3, 2 dc) in next ch-3 sp, (dc in next dc, ch 1, skip
next dc) 3 times, decrease; repeat from ★ across to
last 6 dc, ch 1, skip next dc, (dc in next dc, ch 1, skip
next dc) twice, (2 dc, tr) in last dc: 153 dc.

Row 6: Ch 3, turn; 2 dc in same st, dc in next 2 dc,
ch 1, dc in next dc, ch 1, skip next ch, decrease, ch 1,
dc in next dc, ch 1, ★ dc in next 3 dc, (2 dc, ch 3,
2 dc) in next ch-3 sp, dc in next 3 dc, ch 1, dc in next
dc, ch 1, skip next ch, decrease, ch 1, dc in next dc,
ch 1; repeat from ★ across to last 3 dc, dc in next
2 dc, (2 dc, tr) in last dc: 181 dc.

Rows 7-96: Repeat Rows 3-6, 22 times; then repeat
Rows 3 and 4 once **more**; at end of Row 96, do **not**
finish off.

EDGING

Ch 2, do **not** turn; dc in top of last tr made on Row 96; working in end of rows, (slip st, ch 2, dc) in top of each row across; working in free loops and in sps of beginning ch ***(Fig. 15b, page 140)***, slip st in ch at base of first dc, ch 1, (slip st in next ch-1 sp, ch 1) 3 times, (slip st, ch 3, slip st) in next ch-3 sp, ch 1, (slip st in next ch-1 sp, ch 1) 3 times, † skip next ch, slip st in next ch, ch 1, skip next ch, slip st in sp **before** next ch, ch 1, skip next ch, slip st in next ch, ch 1, (slip st in next ch-1 sp, ch 1) 3 times, (slip st, ch 3, slip st) in next ch-3 sp, ch 1, (slip st in next ch-1 sp, ch 1) 3 times †, repeat from † to † across to last ch, (slip st, ch 2, dc) in last ch; working in end of rows, (slip st, ch 2, dc) in top of each row across to last row, skip last row; working in sts on Row 96, slip st in first dc, ch 3, slip st in next dc, (ch 1, skip next dc, slip st in next dc) 7 times, [ch 1, (slip st, ch 3, slip st) in next ch-3 sp, (ch 1, skip next dc, slip st in next dc) 8 times] across, ch 3; join with slip st at base of beginning ch-2, finish off.

Using ten 16" strands of yarn, add fringe in each point across short edges of Afghan ***(Figs. 22a & c, page 142)***.

FLORAL COMFORT

The granny-style blocks in this comforting afghan resemble dozens of neatly tended flower beds. Simply whipstitch the blocks together and trim with flowing fringe.

Finished Size: 48" x 66"

MATERIALS

Worsted Weight Yarn:
    Rose - 14 ounces, (400 grams, 920 yards)
    Beige - 12 ounces, (340 grams, 790 yards)
    Green - 12 ounces, (340 grams, 790 yards)
    Tan - 10 ounces, (280 grams, 660 yards)
Crochet hook, size H (5.00 mm) **or** size needed for gauge
Yarn needle

GAUGE: Each Block = $6^3/_4$ " x $9^1/_4$ "

STITCH GUIDE

V-STITCH
(Dc, ch 1, dc) in st or sp indicated.

BLOCK (Make 49)

With Rose, ch 13 **loosely**.

Rnd 1 (Right side): 2 Dc in fourth ch from hook, (ch 3, 3 dc in same st) twice, (skip next 2 chs, 3 dc in next ch) twice, skip next 2 chs, 3 dc in last ch, (ch 3, 3 dc in same st) twice; working in free loops of beginning ch *(Fig. 15b, page 140)*, skip next 2 chs, (3 dc in next ch, skip next 2 chs) twice; join with slip st to top of beginning ch, finish off.
Note: Mark Rnd 1 as **right** side.

Rnd 2: With **right** side facing and holding piece vertically, join Beige with slip st in top right corner ch-3 sp; ch 3 **(counts as first dc, now and throughout)**, (2 dc, ch 3, 3 dc) in same sp, (3 dc, ch 3, 3 dc) in next corner ch-3 sp, (skip next 3 dc, 3 dc in sp **before** next 3-dc group) 3 times *(Fig. 18, page 141)*, (3 dc, ch 3, 3 dc) in each of next 2 corner ch-3 sps, (skip next 3 dc, 3 dc in sp **before** next 3-dc group) 3 times; join with slip st to first dc, finish off: 14 3-dc groups.

Rnd 3: With **right** side facing and holding piece vertically, join Green with slip st in top right corner ch-3 sp; ch 3, 2 dc in same sp, skip next 3 dc, 3 dc in sp **before** next 3-dc group, ★ (3 dc, ch 3, 3 dc) in next corner ch-3 sp, (skip next 3 dc, 3 dc in sp **before** next 3-dc group) across to next corner ch-3 sp; repeat from ★ around, 3 dc in same sp as first dc, dc in first dc to form last sp: 18 3-dc groups.

Rnd 4: Ch 3, (2 dc, ch 3, 3 dc) in same sp, (skip next 3 dc, 3 dc in sp **before** next 3-dc group) across to next corner ch-3 sp, ★ (3 dc, ch 3, 3 dc) in corner ch-3 sp, (skip next 3 dc, 3 dc in sp **before** next 3-dc group) across to next corner ch-3 sp; repeat from ★ around; join with slip st to first dc, finish off: 22 3-dc groups.

Rnd 5: With **right** side facing and holding piece vertically, join Beige with slip st in top right corner ch-3 sp; ch 3, (2 dc, ch 3, 3 dc) in same sp, (skip next 3 dc, 3 dc in sp **before** next 3-dc group) across to next corner ch-3 sp, ★ (3 dc, ch 3, 3 dc) in corner ch-3 sp, (skip next 3 dc, 3 dc in sp **before** next 3-dc group) across to next corner ch-3 sp; repeat from ★ around; join with slip st to first dc, finish off: 26 3-dc groups.

Rnd 6: With **right** side facing and holding piece vertically, join Tan with slip st in top right corner ch-3 sp; ch 3, (2 dc, ch 3, 3 dc) in same sp, (skip next 3 dc, 3 dc in sp **before** next 3-dc group) across to next corner ch-3 sp, ★ (3 dc, ch 3, 3 dc) in corner ch-3 sp, (skip next 3 dc, 3 dc in sp **before** next 3-dc group) across to next corner ch-3 sp; repeat from ★ around; join with slip st to first dc, finish off: 30 3-dc groups.

Rnd 7: With **right** side facing and holding piece vertically, join Rose with slip st in top right corner ch-3 sp; ch 4, (dc, ch 2, work V-St) in same sp, work V-St in center dc of each 3-dc group across to next corner ch-3 sp, ★ work (V-St, ch 2, V-St) in corner ch-3 sp, work V-St in center dc of each 3-dc group across to next corner ch-3 sp; repeat from ★ around; join with slip st to third ch of beginning ch-4, finish off: 38 V-Sts.

JOINING

With Rose, working across short ends, and working through **both** loops, whipstitch Blocks together, forming 7 vertical strips of 7 Blocks each *(Fig. 20b, page 142)*, beginning in second ch of first corner ch-2 and ending in first ch of next corner ch-2; then whipstitch strips together.

EDGING

With **right** side facing, join Rose with slip st in any corner ch-2 sp; ch 4, (dc, ch 2, work V-St) in same sp, work V-St in each V-St (ch-1 sp) **and** in each joining between Blocks across to next corner ch-2 sp, ★ work (V-St, ch 2, V-St) in corner ch-2 sp, work V-St in each V-St **and** in each joining between Blocks across to next corner ch-2 sp; repeat from ★ around; join with slip st to third ch of beginning ch-4, finish off.

Add Fringe using 6 strands of Rose *(Figs. 22a & c, page 142)*; attach in each V-St across both short ends of Afghan.

DAINTY DELIGHT

Dainty and lacy — just right for a wee one — our soft and cuddly wrap will make a great gift for a summer baby. Stitch it in any color of baby fingering weight yarn to coordinate with the nursery.

Finished Size: 38" x 48¹/₂ "

MATERIALS
   Baby Fingering Weight Yarn:
      18 ounces, (510 grams, 2,775 yards)
   Crochet hook, size C (2.75 mm) **or** size needed
      for gauge
   Yarn needle

GAUGE: Each Square = 5¹/₄ "

Gauge Swatch: 2¹/₂ " diameter
Work same as Square through Rnd 3.

STITCH GUIDE

CLUSTER (uses next 3 dc)
★ YO, insert hook in **next** dc, YO and pull up a loop, YO and draw through 2 loops on hook; repeat from ★ 2 times **more**, YO and draw through all 4 loops on hook (*Figs. 12a & b, page 139*).

DECREASE (uses next 2 sps)
★ YO, insert hook in **next** sp, YO and pull up a loop, YO and draw through 2 loops on hook; repeat from ★ once **more**, YO and draw through all 3 loops on hook (**counts as one dc**).

PUFF ST (uses one sp)
★ YO, insert hook in sp indicated, YO and pull up a loop, YO and draw through 2 loops on hook; repeat from ★ 2 times **more**, YO and draw through all 4 loops on hook (*Fig. 13, page 139*).

SQUARE (Make 63)

Ch 6; join with slip st to form a ring.
Rnd 1 (Right side): Ch 5, (dc in ring, ch 2) 7 times; join with slip st to third ch of beginning ch-5: 8 ch-2 sps.
Note: Mark Rnd 1 as **right** side.
Rnd 2: Slip st in first ch-2 sp, ch 3 (**counts as first dc, now and throughout**), 2 dc in same sp, (ch 2, 3 dc in next ch-2 sp) around, ch 1, hdc in first dc to form last ch-2 sp: 24 dc and 8 ch-2 sps.
Rnd 3: Ch 6, work Cluster, ch 3, ★ dc in next ch-2 sp, ch 3, work Cluster, ch 3; repeat from ★ around; join with slip st to third ch of beginning ch-6: 8 Clusters and 16 ch-3 sps.

Rnd 4: Slip st in first ch-3 sp, ch 1, sc in same sp, ch 8, sc in next ch-3 sp, ch 5, decrease, ch 5, ★ sc in next ch-3 sp, ch 8, sc in next ch-3 sp, ch 5, decrease, ch 5; repeat from ★ 2 times **more**; join with slip st to first sc: 12 sps.
Rnd 5: In first ch-8 sp work (slip st, ch 4, 3 dc, ch 3, Puff St, ch 3, 3 dc, tr), ch 1, sc in next ch-5 sp, ch 5, sc in next ch-5 sp, ch 1, ★ (tr, 3 dc, ch 3, work Puff St, ch 3, 3 dc, tr) in next ch-8 sp, ch 1, sc in next ch-5 sp, ch 5, sc in next ch-5 sp, ch 1; repeat from ★ 2 times **more**; join with slip st to top of beginning ch-4: 20 sps.
Rnd 6: Slip st in next 2 dc, ch 1, sc in same st, ch 4, (work Puff St in next ch-3 sp, ch 4) twice, skip next dc, sc in next dc, ch 4, skip next ch-1 sp, (2 dc, ch 2, sc, ch 2, 2 dc) in next ch-5 sp, ch 4, skip next ch-1 sp and next 2 sts, ★ sc in next dc, ch 4, (work Puff St in next ch-3 sp, ch 4) twice, skip next dc, sc in next dc, ch 4, skip next ch-1 sp, (2 dc, ch 2, sc, ch 2, 2 dc) in next ch-5 sp, ch 4, skip next ch-1 sp and next 2 sts; repeat from ★ 2 times **more**; join with slip st to first sc: 28 sps.
Rnd 7: Slip st in first ch-4 sp, ch 3, 3 dc in same sp, (dc, ch 4, work Puff St, ch 4, dc) in next ch-4 sp, 4 dc in each of next 2 ch-4 sps, ch 2, decrease, ch 2, ★ 4 dc in each of next 2 ch-4 sps, (dc, ch 4, work Puff St, ch 4, dc) in next ch-4 sp, 4 dc in each of next 2 ch-4 sps, ch 2, decrease, ch 2; repeat from ★ 2 times **more**, 4 dc in last ch-4 sp; join with slip st to first dc: 76 dc and 16 sps.
Rnd 8: Ch 4 (**counts as first dc plus ch 1**), (skip next dc, dc in next dc, ch 1) twice, (dc, ch 1) twice in next ch-4 sp, (tr, ch 1) twice in next Puff St (corner made), (dc, ch 1) twice in next ch-4 sp, dc in next dc, ch 1, (skip next dc, dc in next dc, ch 1) 4 times, (dc in next ch-2 sp, ch 1) twice, ★ dc in next dc, ch 1, (skip next dc, dc in next dc, ch 1) 4 times, (dc, ch 1) twice in next ch-4 sp, (tr, ch 1) twice in next Puff St (corner made), (dc, ch 1) twice in next ch-4 sp, dc in next dc, ch 1, (skip next dc, dc in next dc, ch 1) 4 times, (dc in next ch-2 sp, ch 1) twice; repeat from ★ 2 times **more**, (dc in next dc, ch 1, skip next dc) twice; join with slip st to first dc, finish off: 72 sts and 72 ch-1 sps.

ASSEMBLY

Working through **both** loops, whipstitch Squares together forming 7 vertical strips of 9 Squares each *(Fig. 20b, page 142)*, beginning in center ch-1 of first corner and ending in center ch-1 of next corner; then whipstitch strips together in same manner.

EDGING

Rnd 1: With **right** side of short edge facing, join yarn with slip st in right corner ch-1 sp; ch 6, dc in same sp, ch 1, ★ (dc in next sp, ch 1) across to next corner ch-1 sp, (dc, ch 3, dc) in corner sp, ch 1; repeat from ★ 2 times **more**, (dc in next sp, ch 1) across; join with slip st to third ch of beginning ch-6: 608 sts and 608 sps.

Rnd 2: Ch 1, sc in same st, † ch 3, work Puff St in corner ch-3 sp, ch 3, sc in next dc, ch 3, [YO, insert hook in next dc, YO and pull up a loop, YO and draw through 2 loops on hook, YO, insert hook in next ch-1 sp, YO and pull up a loop, YO and draw through 2 loops on hook, YO, insert hook in next dc, YO and pull up a loop, YO and draw through 2 loops on hook, YO and draw through all 4 loops on hook, ch 3, sc in next dc, ch 3] across to next corner ch-3 sp, work Puff St in corner ch-3 sp, ch 3, sc in next dc, ch 3, YO, insert hook in next ch-1 sp, YO and pull up a loop, YO and draw through 2 loops on hook, YO, insert hook in next dc, YO and pull up a loop, YO and draw through 2 loops on hook, YO, insert hook in next ch-1 sp, YO and pull up a loop, YO and draw through 2 loops on hook, YO and draw through all 4 loops on hook, ch 3, [sc in next ch-1 sp, ch 3, YO, insert hook in next ch-1 sp, YO and pull up a loop, YO and draw through 2 loops on hook, YO, insert hook in next dc, YO and pull up a loop, YO and draw through 2 loops on hook, YO, insert hook in next ch-1 sp, YO and pull up a loop, YO and draw through 2 loops on hook, YO and draw through all 4 loops on hook, ch 3] across to next corner ch-3 sp †, sc in next dc, repeat from † to † once; join with slip st to first sc, finish off.

MORNING GLORY

A simple lattice-look background sets off glorious trailing flowers on this delicate wrap. The lovely creation will make a nice gift to nurture a blossoming friendship.

Finished Size: 48" x 66"

MATERIALS
  Worsted Weight Yarn:
    White - 33 ounces, (940 grams, 2,265 yards)
    Blue - 3 ounces, (90 grams, 205 yards)
    Green - 3 ounces, (90 grams, 205 yards)
  Crochet hooks, sizes H (5.00 mm) **and**
    I (5.50 mm) **or** sizes needed for gauge
  Yarn needle

GAUGE: With smaller size hook,
      14 dc = 4" and 6 rows = 3"

STITCH GUIDE

HALF TREBLE CROCHET *(abbreviated htr)*
YO twice, insert hook in st indicated, YO and pull up a loop, YO and draw through first 2 loops on hook, YO and draw through remaining 3 loops on hook.
DECREASE (uses next 2 sts)
★ YO, insert hook in **next** st, YO and pull up a loop, YO and draw through 2 loops on hook; repeat from ★ once **more**, YO and draw through all 3 loops on hook **(counts as one dc)**.

Note: Afghan is worked from side to side.

AFGHAN BODY

With White and smaller size hook, ch 219 **loosely**.
Row 1: Dc in fourth ch from **hook (3 skipped chs count as first dc)** and in each ch across: 217 dc.
Row 2 (Right side): Ch 3 **(counts as first dc, now and throughout)**, turn; dc in next dc and in each dc across.
Note: Mark Row 2 as **right** side.
Rows 3-6: Ch 3, turn; dc in next dc and in each dc across.
Row 7: Ch 1, turn; sc in first 3 dc, ★ † hdc in next 2 dc, dc in next 2 dc, htr in next 2 dc, tr in next 2 dc, htr in next 2 dc, dc in next 2 dc, hdc in next 2 dc †, sc in next 4 dc; repeat from ★ 10 times **more**, then repeat from † to † once, sc in last 2 dc.

Row 8: Ch 1, turn; sc in first 2 sc, ★ † hdc in next 2 hdc, dc in next 2 dc, htr in next 2 htr, tr in next 2 tr, htr in next 2 htr, dc in next 2 dc, hdc in next 2 hdc †, sc in next 4 sc; repeat from ★ 10 times **more**, then repeat from † to † once, sc in last 3 sc; finish off.
Row 9: With **right** side facing and smaller size hook, join Green with slip st in first sc; ch 2 **(counts as first hdc)**, decrease, hdc in next 5 sts, 2 hdc in each of next 2 tr, ★ hdc in next 6 sts, decrease twice, hdc in next 6 sts, 2 hdc in each of next 2 tr; repeat from ★ 10 times **more**, hdc in next 5 sts, decrease, hdc in last 2 sc; finish off.
Row 10: With **right** side facing and smaller size hook, join White with slip st in first hdc; ch 4 **(counts as first tr, now and throughout)**, htr in next 2 sts, ★ † dc in next 2 hdc, hdc in next 2 hdc, sc in next 4 hdc, hdc in next 2 hdc, dc in next 2 hdc †, htr in next 2 hdc, tr in next 2 dc, htr in next 2 hdc; repeat from ★ 10 times **more**, then repeat from † to † once, htr in next 3 sts, tr in last hdc.
Row 11: Ch 4, turn; htr in next 3 htr, ★ † dc in next 2 dc, hdc in next 2 hdc, sc in next 4 sc, hdc in next 2 hdc, dc in next 2 dc, htr in next 2 htr †, tr in next 2 tr, htr in next 2 htr; repeat from ★ 10 times **more**, then repeat from † to † once, tr in last tr.
Rows 12-17: Ch 3, turn; dc in next st and in each st across.
Change to larger size hook.
Row 18: Ch 5, turn; skip first 3 dc, slip st in next dc, (ch 5, skip next 2 dc, slip st in next dc) across: 72 loops.
Rows 19-35: Ch 5, turn; slip st in center ch of first loop, (ch 5, slip st in center ch of next loop) across.
Row 36: Ch 5, turn; slip st in center ch of first loop, (ch 3, slip st in center ch of next loop) across.
Change to smaller size hook.
Row 37: Ch 3, turn; dc in next 3 chs, (skip next slip st, dc in next 3 chs) across to last 2 chs, leave remaining chs unworked: 217 dc.
Row 38: Ch 3, turn; dc in next dc and in each dc across.
Rows 39-89: Repeat Rows 3-38 once, then repeat Rows 3-17 once **more**.
Do **not** finish off.

Continued on page 70.

EDGING

Rnd 1: With smaller size hook, ch 4, turn; 2 dc in same st, dc in each dc across to last dc, (2 dc, ch 1, 2 dc) in last dc; work 155 dc evenly spaced across end of rows; working in free loops of beginning ch *(Fig. 15b, page 140)*, (2 dc, ch 1, 2 dc) in ch at base of first dc, dc in each ch across to last ch, (2 dc, ch 1, 2 dc) in last ch; work 155 dc evenly spaced across end of rows; dc in same st as beginning ch; join with slip st to third ch of beginning ch-4: 756 sts and 4 ch-1 sps.
Rnd 2: Slip st in first ch-1 sp, ch 1, (sc in same sp, ch 5) twice, ★ skip next dc, (sc in next dc, ch 5, skip next dc) across to next ch-1 sp, (sc, ch 5) twice in ch-1 sp; repeat from ★ 2 times **more**, skip next dc, (sc in next dc, ch 5, skip next st) across; join with slip st to first sc.
Rnd 3: Slip st in first 3 chs, ch 1, sc in same st, ch 5, (sc in center ch of next loop, ch 5) around; join with slip st to first sc, finish off.

FLOWERS (Make 24)

With Blue and smaller size hook, ch 23 **loosely**; being careful not to twist ch, join with slip st to form a ring.
Rnd 1 (Right side): Ch 3, skip next ch, decrease, (dc in next ch, decrease) 6 times, skip last ch; join with slip st to first dc: 14 dc.
Rnds 2-6: Ch 3, decrease, dc in next dc and in each dc around to last 2 dc, decrease; join with slip st to first dc.
Finish off.

LEAVES (Make 21)

With Green and smaller size hook, ch 10 **loosely**.
Rnd 1 (Right side): Slip st in second ch from hook and in next ch, sc in next ch, hdc in next ch, dc in next ch, htr in next 2 chs, tr in next ch, (4 tr, ch 4, slip st, ch 4, 4 tr) in last ch; working in free loops of beginning ch, tr in next ch, htr in next 2 chs, dc in next ch, hdc in next ch, sc in next ch, slip st in next 2 chs; finish off.

FINISHING

Using photo as a guide for placement:
Turn down upper edge of each Flower and tack in place; sew Flowers and Leaves to Afghan.
With White, add accent lines to each Flower.

DAZZLING DIAMONDS

Sparkling like gemstones, this afghan will make a precious addition to your collection of fine things. Cluster stitches form the dazzling diamond pattern.

Finished Size: 53" x 74"

MATERIALS
Worsted Weight Yarn:
Ecru - 51 ounces, (1,450 grams, 3,495 yards)
Blue - 29 ounces, (820 grams, 1,990 yards)
Crochet hook, size I (5.50 mm) **or** size needed for gauge
Safety pin
Yarn needle

GAUGE: Each Square = 5^1/$_4$ "

Gauge Swatch: 3" square
Work same as Square through Rnd 3.

STITCH GUIDE

CLUSTER (uses one ch)
Ch 3, YO, insert hook in third ch from hook, YO and pull up a loop, YO and draw through 2 loops on hook, YO, insert hook in same ch, YO and pull up a loop, YO and draw through 2 loops on hook, YO and draw through all 3 loops on hook *(Figs. 11a & b, page 139)*.

SQUARE (Make 117)
Rnd 1 (Right side): With Ecru, ch 4, 2 dc in fourth ch from hook **(3 skipped chs count as first dc)**, ch 3, (3 dc in same ch, ch 3) 3 times; join with slip st to first dc, place loop from hook onto safety pin to keep piece from unraveling as you work the next rnd: 12 dc and 4 ch-3 sps.
Note: Mark Rnd 1 as **right** side.
Hold safety pin and dropped loop on **wrong** side, **now and throughout**.
Rnd 2: With **wrong** side facing, join Blue with sc in any ch-3 sp *(see Joining With Sc, page 140)*; ch 3, sc in same sp, work Cluster, ch 1, skip next 3 dc, ★ (sc, ch 3, sc) in next ch-3 sp, work Cluster, ch 1, skip next 3 dc; repeat from ★ 2 times **more**; join with slip st to first sc, finish off: 4 Clusters, 8 sc, and 4 ch-3 sps.
Rnd 3: With **right** side facing and working **behind** Rnd 2 *(Fig. 16, page 141)*, remove safety pin and place loop onto hook; ch 3 **(counts as first dc, now and throughout)**, dc in next 2 skipped dc on Rnd 1, ★ † sc in next sc on Rnd 2, working in **front** of next ch-3, (dc, ch 3, dc) in ch-3 sp on Rnd 1 **before** next sc, sc in next sc on Rnd 2 †, working **behind** next Cluster, dc in next 3 skipped dc on Rnd 1; repeat from ★ 2 times **more**, then repeat from † to † once; join with slip st to first dc, place loop from hook onto safety pin to keep piece from unraveling as you work the next rnd: 28 sts and 4 ch-3 sps.
Rnd 4: With **wrong** side facing, join Blue with sc in any corner ch-3 sp; ch 3, sc in same sp, work Cluster, ch 1, skip next 3 sts, sc in next dc, work Cluster, ch 1, skip next 3 sts, ★ (sc, ch 3, sc) in next corner ch-3 sp, work Cluster, ch 1, skip next 3 sts, sc in next dc, work Cluster, ch 1, skip next 3 sts; repeat from ★ 2 times **more**; join with slip st to first sc, finish off: 8 Clusters, 12 sc, and 4 ch-3 sps.

Continued on page 72.

Rnd 5: With **right** side facing and working **behind** Rnd 4, remove safety pin and place loop onto hook; ch 3, sc in next sc on Rnd 4, working **behind** next Cluster, dc in next 3 skipped sts on Rnd 3, sc in next sc on Rnd 4, working in **front** of next ch-3, (dc, ch 3, dc) in ch-3 sp on Rnd 3 **before** next sc, sc in next sc on Rnd 4, ★ (working **behind** next Cluster, dc in next 3 skipped sts on Rnd 3, sc in next sc on Rnd 4) twice, working in **front** of next ch-3, (dc, ch 3, dc) in ch-3 sp on Rnd 3 **before** next sc, sc in next sc on Rnd 4; repeat from ★ 2 times **more**, working **behind** last Cluster, dc in last 2 skipped sts on Rnd 3; join with slip st to first dc, place loop from hook onto safety pin to keep piece from unraveling as you work the next rnd: 44 sts and 4 ch-3 sps.

Rnd 6: With **wrong** side facing, join Blue with sc in any corner ch-3 sp; ch 3, sc in same sp, ★ † (ch 1, skip next dc, sc in next st) twice, work Cluster, ch 1, skip next 3 sts, (sc in next st, ch 1, skip next dc) twice †, (sc, ch 3, sc) in next corner ch-3 sp; repeat from ★ 2 times **more**, then repeat from † to † once; join with slip st to first sc, finish off: 4 Clusters, 24 sc, and 4 ch-3 sps.

Rnd 7: With **right** side facing and working **behind** Rnd 6, remove safety pin and place loop onto hook; ch 3, dc in next 2 skipped sts on Rnd 5, sc in next sc on Rnd 6, ★ † (working in **front** of next ch-1, dc in next skipped dc on Rnd 5, sc in next sc on Rnd 6) twice, working in **front** of next ch-3, (dc, ch 3, dc) in ch-3 sp on Rnd 5 **before** next sc, sc in next sc on Rnd 6, (working in **front** of next ch-1, dc in next skipped dc on Rnd 5, sc in next sc on Rnd 6) twice †, working **behind** next Cluster, dc in next 3 skipped sts on Rnd 5, sc in next sc on Rnd 6; repeat from ★ 2 times **more**, then repeat from † to † once; join with slip st to first dc, finish off: 60 sts and 4 ch-3 sps.

ASSEMBLY

With Ecru and working through **both** loops, whipstitch Squares together forming 9 vertical strips of 13 Squares each *(Fig. 20b, page 142)*, beginning in center ch of first corner ch-3 and ending in center ch of next corner ch-3; then whipstitch strips together in same manner.

EDGING

Rnd 1: With **right** side facing, join Ecru with slip st in any corner ch-3 sp; ch 3, (dc, ch 3, 2 dc) in same sp, ★ † dc in next 15 sts, [dc in top 2 loops of next ch *(Fig. 1)* and in next joining, dc in top 2 loops of next ch and in next 15 sts] across to next corner ch-3 sp †, (2 dc, ch 3, 2 dc) in corner ch-3 sp; repeat from ★ 2 times **more**, then repeat from † to † once; join with slip st to first dc, finish off: 796 dc and 4 ch-3 sps.

Fig. 1

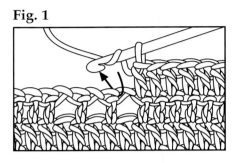

Rnd 2: With **wrong** side facing, join Blue with sc in any corner ch-3 sp; work Cluster, ch 1, sc in same sp, ★ † work Cluster, ch 1, skip next 3 sts, (sc in next st, work Cluster, ch 1, skip next 3 sts) across to next corner ch-3 sp †, (sc, work Cluster, ch 1, sc) in corner ch-3 sp; repeat from ★ 2 times **more**, then repeat from † to † once; join with slip st to first sc, finish off: 204 Clusters.

Rnd 3: With **right** side facing, join Ecru with sc in sc after any corner Cluster; ★ † (working **behind** next Cluster, dc in next 3 skipped sts one rnd **below** Cluster, sc in next sc) across to next corner Cluster, working **behind** corner Cluster, (dc, ch 3, dc) in ch-3 sp **before** next sc one rnd **below** Cluster †, sc in next sc; repeat from ★ 2 times **more**, then repeat from † to † once; join with slip st to first sc, finish off: 812 sts and 4 ch-3 sps.

Rnds 4-7: Repeat Rnds 2 and 3 twice; at end of Rnd 7, do **not** finish off: 844 sts and 4 ch-3 sps.

Rnd 8: Ch 1, sc in same st, ch 1, skip next dc, ★ (sc in next st, ch 1, skip next st) across to next corner ch-3 sp, (sc, ch 2, sc) in corner ch-3 sp, ch 1, skip next dc; repeat from ★ around; join with slip st to first sc.

Rnd 9: Slip st in next ch-1 sp, ch 1, ★ (slip st in next ch-1 sp, ch 1) across to next corner ch-2 sp, (slip st, ch 2, slip st) in corner ch-2 sp, ch 1; repeat from ★ around to last ch-1 sp, slip st in last ch-1 sp, ch 1; join with slip st to first slip st, finish off.

AUTUMN

Displaying its vibrant hues of red, gold, and orange, autumn arrives with great splendor. It stirs the souls and warms the hearts of everyone who takes the time to enjoy the glory of this dazzling season. Created with chilly fall weather in mind, the hearty throws in this stylish collection will wrap you and your loved ones in colorful comfort.

TIMELESS FAVORITE

If you're wild about classic designs, you'll love this afghan celebrating the awesome beauty of the jaguar. This timeless throw is destined to be a favorite.

Finished Size: 47¹/₂" x 63¹/₂"

MATERIALS
Worsted Weight Yarn:
Tan - 40 ounces, (1,140 grams, 2,260 yards)
Black - 9 ounces, (260 grams, 510 yards)
Brown - 4 ounces, (110 grams, 225 yards)
Crochet hook, size I (5.50 mm) **or** size needed for gauge
Yarn needle

GAUGE SWATCH: 4" square
Work same as Square.

SQUARE (Make 165)
With Brown, ch 5 **loosely**.
Rnd 1 (Right side): Hdc in third ch from hook **(2 skipped chs count as first hdc)** and in next ch, 3 hdc in last ch; working in free loops of beginning ch *(Fig. 15b, page 140)*, hdc in next 2 chs, 2 hdc in next ch; join with slip st to first hdc, finish off: 10 hdc.
Note: Mark Rnd 1 as **right** side.
Rnd 2: With **right** side facing, join Black with sc in same st as joining *(see Joining With Sc, page 140)*; sc in same st and in next 2 hdc, 2 sc in each of next 3 hdc, sc in next 2 hdc, 2 sc in each of last 2 hdc; join with slip st to first sc, finish off: 16 sc.
Rnd 3: With **right** side facing, join Tan with slip st in first sc to left of joining; ch 3 **(counts as first dc, now and throughout)**, (dc, ch 2, 2 dc) in same st, ch 1, skip next sc, 3 dc in next sc, ch 1, skip next sc, ★ (2 dc, ch 2, 2 dc) in next sc, ch 1, skip next sc, 3 dc in next sc, ch 1, skip next sc; repeat from ★ 2 times **more**; join with slip st to first dc, do **not** finish off: 28 dc and 12 sps.

Rnd 4: Slip st in next dc and in next ch-2 sp, ch 3, (dc, ch 3, 2 dc) in same sp, ch 1, (3 dc in next ch-1 sp, ch 1) twice, ★ (2 dc, ch 3, 2 dc) in next ch-2 sp, ch 1, (3 dc in next ch-1 sp, ch 1) twice; repeat from ★ 2 times **more**; join with slip st to first dc, finish off: 40 dc and 16 sps.

ASSEMBLY
With Tan, using photo as a guide for placement, and working through **inside** loops, whipstitch Squares together forming 11 vertical strips of 15 Squares each *(Fig. 20a, page 142)*, beginning in center ch of first corner ch-3 and ending in center ch of next corner ch-3; then whipstitch strips together in same manner.

EDGING
Rnd 1: With **right** side facing, join Black with slip st in any corner ch-3 sp; ch 3, (dc, ch 2, 2 dc) in same sp, ch 1, (2 dc in next sp, ch 1) across to next corner ch-3 sp, ★ (2 dc, ch 2, 2 dc) in corner ch-3 sp, ch 1, (2 dc in next sp, ch 1) across to next corner ch-3 sp; repeat from ★ 2 times **more**; join with slip st to first dc, finish off: 260 sps.
Rnd 2: With **right** side facing, join Brown with slip st in any corner ch-2 sp; ch 3, (dc, ch 2, 2 dc) in same sp, ch 1, (2 dc in next ch-1 sp, ch 1) across to next corner ch-2 sp, ★ (2 dc, ch 2, 2 dc) in corner ch-2 sp, ch 1, (2 dc in next ch-1 sp, ch 1) across to next corner ch-2 sp; repeat from ★ 2 times **more**; join with slip st to first dc, finish off.
Rnd 3: With Black, repeat Rnd 2.

HONEYCOMB

Plush and comfy, this beautiful fall warmer is ideal for evenings at home. Lacy edging enhances the elegance of the deeply textured honeycomb design.

Finished Size: 46" x 60¼"

MATERIALS
Brushed Acrylic Worsted Weight Yarn:
62 ounces, (1,760 grams, 3,140 yards)
Crochet hook, size J (6.00 mm) **or** size needed for gauge

GAUGE: In pattern, (Cluster, 2 sc) 3 times = 3½";
10 rows = 3¾"

Gauge Swatch: 4"w x 3¾"h
Ch 12 **loosely.**
Work same as Afghan Body for 10 rows.
Finish off.

STITCH GUIDE

CLUSTER (uses one sc)
★ YO, insert hook in sc indicated, YO and pull up a loop, YO and draw through 2 loops on hook; repeat from ★ 4 times **more**, YO and draw through all 6 loops on hook *(Figs. 11a & b, page 139)*. Push Cluster to **right** side.

AFGHAN BODY
Ch 108 **loosely.**
Row 1: Sc in second ch from hook and in each ch across: 107 sc.
Row 2 (Right side)**:** Ch 1, turn; sc in first sc, work Cluster in next sc, (sc in next 2 sc, work Cluster in next sc) across to last 3 sc, sc in last 3 sc: 35 Clusters and 72 sc.
Row 3: Ch 1, turn; sc in each st across: 107 sc.
Row 4: Ch 1, turn; sc in first 2 sc, (work Cluster in next sc, sc in next 2 sc) across: 35 Clusters and 72 sc.
Row 5: Ch 1, turn; sc in each st across: 107 sc.
Row 6: Ch 1, turn; sc in first sc, work Cluster in next sc, (sc in next 2 sc, work Cluster in next sc) across to last 3 sc, sc in last 3 sc: 35 Clusters and 72 sc.
Rows 7-147: Repeat Rows 3-6, 35 times; then repeat Row 3 once **more**; do **not** finish off.

EDGING
Rnd 1: Ch 1, turn; 2 sc in first sc, sc in next sc and in each sc across to last sc, 3 sc in last sc; sc in end of each row across; working in free loops of beginning ch *(Fig. 15b, page 140)*, 3 sc in ch at base of first sc, sc in next ch and each ch across to last ch, 3 sc in last ch; sc in end of each row across and in same st as first sc; join with slip st to first sc: 516 sc.
Rnd 2: Ch 13, do **not** turn; tr in same st, ch 1, skip next 2 sc, sc in next sc, ch 1, skip next 2 sc, ★ (tr, ch 9, tr) in next sc, ch 1, skip next 2 sc, sc in next sc, ch 1, skip next 2 sc; repeat from ★ around; join with slip st to fourth ch of beginning ch-13: 86 ch-9 sps.
Rnd 3: Ch 2, (4 dc, ch 5, 4 dc) in next ch-9 sp, hdc in next tr, sc in next ch-1 sp, work Cluster in next sc; sc in next ch-1 sp, ★ hdc in next tr, [(4 dc, ch 3, 4 dc) in next ch-9 sp, hdc in next tr, sc in next ch-1 sp, work Cluster in next sc, sc in next ch-1 sp, hdc in next tr] across to next corner ch-9 sp, (4 dc, ch 5, 4 dc) in corner ch-9 sp, hdc in next tr, sc in next ch-1 sp, work Cluster in next sc, sc in next ch-1 sp; repeat from ★ 2 times **more**, [hdc in next tr, (4 dc, ch 3, 4 dc) in next ch-9 sp, hdc in next tr, sc in next ch-1 sp, work Cluster in next sc, sc in next ch-1 sp] across; join with slip st to top of beginning ch-2, finish off.

BREEZY STRIPES

Colorful stripes set off by rows of black make this wrap a striking addition to your décor. Some of the fringe is created as you go, since you leave long ends when joining and finishing off.

Finished Size: 47$^1/_2$" x 60"

MATERIALS
Worsted Weight Yarn:
  Black - 12$^1/_2$ ounces, (360 grams, 705 yards)
  Lt Rose - 11 ounces, (310 grams, 620 yards)
  Lt Green - 10$^1/_2$ ounces, (300 grams, 595 yards)
  Dk Rose - 6 ounces, (170 grams, 340 yards)
  Dk Green - 5$^1/_2$ ounces, (160 grams, 310 yards)
  Ecru - 5 ounces, (140 grams, 285 yards)
  Yellow - 5 ounces, (140 grams, 285 yards)
Crochet hook, size I (5.50 mm) **or** size needed
  for gauge

GAUGE: In pattern, (sc, ch 1) 8 times = 4";
        11 rows = 3"

Gauge Swatch: 3$^3/_4$"w x 3"h
With Black, ch 16.
Work same as Afghan Body for 11 rows.

COLOR SEQUENCE
One row **each:** ★ † Black, Lt Rose, Dk Rose, Lt Rose, Black, Lt Green, Dk Green, Lt Green, Black, Lt Rose, Dk Rose, Lt Rose, Black †, Ecru, Yellow, Lt Green, Dk Green, Lt Green, Yellow, Ecru; repeat from ★ 7 times **more**, then repeat from † to † once.

AFGHAN BODY
With Black, ch 240.
Row 1 (Wrong side): Sc in second ch from hook, ★ ch 1, skip next ch, sc in next ch; repeat from ★ across; finish off: 120 sc and 119 ch-1 sps.
Note: Mark Row 1 as **right** side.
Row 2: With **right** side facing, join next color with sc in first sc *(see Joining With Sc, page 140)*; (ch 1, sc in next sc) across; finish off.
Row 3: With **wrong** side facing, join next color with sc in first sc; (ch 1, sc in next sc) across; finish off.
Rows 4-173: Repeat Rows 2 and 3, 85 times.

TRIM
FIRST SIDE
With **right** side facing, join Black with slip st in first sc on Row 173; (slip st in next ch-1 sp, ch 1) across to last ch-1 sp, slip st in last ch-1 sp and in last sc; finish off.

SECOND SIDE
With **right** side facing, working in free loops *(Fig. 15b, page 140)* and in sps across beginning ch, join Black with slip st in ch at base of first sc; (slip st in next sp, ch 1) across to last sp, slip st in last sp and in last ch; finish off.

Holding 2 strands of corresponding color yarn together, add additional fringe in each row across short edges of Afghan *(Figs. 22b & d, page 142)*.

GOLDEN HARVEST

Cuddle up with the harvest of color in this gorgeous afghan.
Each square uses a bumper crop of beautiful stitches.

Finished Size: 46" x 61"

MATERIALS
Worsted Weight Yarn:
    Gold - 8$\frac{1}{2}$ ounces, (240 grams, 560 yards)
    Ecru - 9$\frac{1}{2}$ ounces, (270 grams, 625 yards)
    Dk Green - 11 ounces, (310 grams, 725 yards)
    Green - 17$\frac{1}{2}$ ounces, (500 grams, 1,150 yards)
Crochet hook, size I (5.50 mm) **or** size needed
    for gauge
Yarn needle

GAUGE: Each Square = 5"

STITCH GUIDE

> **LONG DOUBLE CROCHET** *(abbreviated LDC)*
> YO, working **around** Rnd 4 *(Fig. 16, page 141)*,
> insert hook in next st one rnd **below** next dc, YO
> and pull up a loop even with last st made, (YO
> and draw through 2 loops on hook) twice *(Fig. 9,
> page 139)*.

SQUARE (Make 108)

Rnd 1 (Right side): With Gold, ch 4, 2 dc in fourth
ch from hook, ch 2, (3 dc in same st, ch 2) 3 times;
join with slip st to top of beginning ch: 4 ch-2 sps.
Note: Mark Rnd 1 as **right** side.

Rnd 2: Slip st in next dc, ch 3 **(counts as first dc,
now and throughout)**, (2 dc, ch 2, 3 dc) in same st,
sc in next ch-2 sp, ★ skip next dc, (3 dc, ch 2, 3 dc) in
next dc, sc in next ch-2 sp; repeat from ★ around;
join with slip st to first dc, finish off: 28 sts and
4 ch-2 sps.

Rnd 3: With **right** side facing, join Ecru with slip st
in any ch-2 sp; ch 1, sc in same sp, hdc in next dc, dc
in next dc, tr in next dc, (dtr, ch 3, dtr) in next sc
(corner made), tr in next dc, dc in next dc, hdc in
next dc, ★ sc in next ch-2 sp, hdc in next dc, dc in
next dc, tr in next dc, (dtr, ch 3, dtr) in next sc
(corner made), tr in next dc, dc in next dc, hdc in
next dc; repeat from ★ around; join with slip st to
first sc, finish off: 36 sts and 4 ch-3 sps.

Rnd 4: With **right** side facing, join Dk Green with
slip st in any corner ch-3 sp; ch 3, (dc, ch 3, 2 dc) in
same sp, dc in next 9 sts, ★ (2 dc, ch 3, 2 dc) in next
corner ch-3 sp, dc in next 9 sts; repeat from ★
around; join with slip st to first dc, finish off: 52 dc
and 4 ch-3 sps.

Rnd 5: With **right** side facing, join Green with slip st
in any corner ch-3 sp; ch 1, (sc, ch 3, sc) in same sp,
sc in next 2 dc, work LDC, (sc in next dc, work
LDC) 4 times, sc in next 2 dc, ★ (sc, ch 3, sc) in next
corner ch-3 sp, sc in next 2 dc, work LDC, (sc in next
dc, work LDC) 4 times, sc in next 2 dc; repeat from
★ around; join with slip st to first sc, finish off: 60 sts
and 4 ch-3 sps.

ASSEMBLY

With Green and working through **both** loops,
whipstitch Squares together forming 9 vertical strips
of 12 Squares each *(Fig. 20, page 142)*, beginning in
center ch of first corner and ending in center ch of
next corner; then whipstitch strips together in same
manner.

EDGING

With **right** side facing, join Green with slip st in any
st; ch 1, sc evenly around working (sc, ch 3, sc) in
each corner ch-3 sp; join with slip st to first sc,
finish off.

Using four 18" lengths of Green held together, attach
fringe in each ch-3 sp and in every third sc across
both ends of Afghan *(Figs. 22a & c, page 142)*.

TOASTY EARTH TONES

In toasty autumn shades, this throw will warm you — heart and soul.
It's a breeze to work in simple rows, then finish with tasseled fringe.

Finished Size: 48" x 65"

MATERIALS
Worsted Weight Yarn:
Ecru - 20¼ ounces, (580 grams, 980 yards)
Brown - 19 ounces, (540 grams, 920 yards)
Gold - 19 ounces, (540 grams, 920 yards)
Crochet hook, size I (5.50 mm) **or** size needed
for gauge

GAUGE: In pattern, from point to point = 6";
8 rows = 4"

Gauge Swatch: 12"w x 4"h
Ch 51 **loosely**.
Work same as Afghan for 8 rows.

STITCH GUIDE

LONG DOUBLE CROCHET *(abbreviated LDC)*
YO, working **around** next ch-1 *(Fig. 16, page 141)*, insert hook in skipped dc one row **below** ch-1, YO and pull up a loop even with loop on hook (3 loops on hook), (YO and draw through 2 loops on hook) twice *(Fig. 9, page 139)*.
SINGLE CROCHET DECREASE
(abbreviated sc decrease)
Pull up a loop in next 2 sts, YO and draw through all 3 loops on hook.
DOUBLE CROCHET DECREASE
(abbreviated dc decrease) (uses next 2 sts)
★ YO, insert hook in **next** st or ch, YO and pull up a loop, YO and draw through 2 loops on hook; repeat from ★ once **more**, YO and draw through all 3 loops on hook.

AFGHAN

With Ecru, ch 213 **loosely**.
Row 1 (Right side): Working in back ridges of beginning ch *(Fig. 2b, page 137)*, dc in third ch from hook and in next 9 chs, (dc, ch 3, dc) in next ch, ★ dc in next 11 chs, skip next 4 chs, dc in next 11 chs, (dc, ch 3, dc) in next ch; repeat from ★ across to last 11 chs, dc in next 9 chs, dc decrease: 190 sts and 8 ch-3 sps.
Note: Mark Row 1 as **right** side.

Rows 2 and 3: Ch 2, turn; skip first st, dc in next 10 dc, (dc, ch 3, dc) in next ch-3 sp, ★ dc in next 10 dc, dc decrease twice, dc in next 10 dc, (dc, ch 3, dc) in next ch-3 sp; repeat from ★ across to last 11 sts, dc in next 9 dc, dc decrease.
Row 4: Ch 2, turn; skip first st, (dc in next dc, ch 1, skip next dc) 5 times, (dc, ch 3, dc) in next ch-3 sp, ★ (ch 1, skip next dc, dc in next dc) 5 times, dc decrease twice, (dc in next dc, ch 1, skip next dc) 5 times, (dc, ch 3, dc) in next ch-3 sp; repeat from ★ across to last 11 sts, ch 1, skip next dc, (dc in next dc, ch 1, skip next dc) 4 times, dc decrease; finish off: 110 sts and 88 sps.
Row 5: With **right** side facing and using Gold, insert hook in first st, YO and pull up a loop, YO, working **around** next ch-1, insert hook in skipped dc one row **below** ch-1, YO and pull up a loop even with loop on hook, YO and draw through 2 loops on hook, YO and draw through all 3 loops on hook, sc in next dc, (work LDC, sc in next dc) 4 times, (sc, ch 3, sc) in next ch-3 sp, ★ (sc in next dc, work LDC) 5 times, sc decrease twice, (work LDC, sc in next dc) 5 times, (sc, ch 3, sc) in next ch-3 sp; repeat from ★ across to last 5 ch-1 sps, sc in next dc, (work LDC, sc in next dc) 4 times, YO, working **around** next ch-1, insert hook in skipped dc one row **below** ch-1, YO and pull up a loop even with loop on hook, YO and draw through 2 loops on hook, insert hook in last st, YO and pull up a loop, YO and draw through all 3 loops on hook: 190 sts and 8 ch-3 sps.
Rows 6 and 7: Ch 2, turn; skip first st, dc in next 10 sts, (dc, ch 3, dc) in next ch-3 sp, ★ dc in next 10 sts, dc decrease twice, dc in next 10 sts, (dc, ch 3, dc) in next ch-3 sp; repeat from ★ across to last 11 sts, dc in next 9 sts, dc decrease.
Row 8: Ch 2, turn; skip first st, (dc in next dc, ch 1, skip next dc) 5 times, (dc, ch 3, dc) in next ch-3 sp, ★ (ch 1, skip next dc, dc in next dc) 5 times, dc decrease twice, (dc in next dc, ch 1, skip next dc) 5 times, (dc, ch 3, dc) in next ch-3 sp; repeat from ★ across to last 11 sts, ch 1, skip next dc, (dc in next dc, ch 1, skip next dc) 4 times, dc decrease; finish off: 110 sts and 88 sps.
Rows 9-12: With Brown, repeat Rows 5-8.
Rows 13-16: With Ecru, repeat Rows 5-8.
Rows 17-124: Repeat Rows 5-16, 9 times.

Holding 10 strands of Ecru yarn together, each 16" long, add fringe in each point across short edges of Afghan *(Figs. 22a & c, page 142)*.

FALL PORTRAIT

*With each block resembling a portrait of vibrant autumn leaves, our cozy afghan
is sure to become one of your favorites. You'll enjoy the warmth
of this worsted weight wrap for many years to come.*

Finished Size: 53" x 70"

MATERIALS
 Worsted Weight Yarn:
  Ecru - 8 ounces, (230 grams, 525 yards)
  Tan - 11 ounces, (310 grams, 725 yards)
  Rust - 8 ounces, (230 grams, 525 yards)
  Green - 23 ounces, (650 grams, 1,515 yards)
 Crochet hook, size I (5.50 mm) **or** size needed
  for gauge
 Yarn needle

GAUGE: Rnds 1-5 = 4"
    Each Square = $8^1/_2$"

SQUARE (Make 48)
Note: The completed Square will jog to the left. This
is a characteristic of the design and cannot be
avoided.

With Ecru, ch 4; join with slip st to form a ring.
Rnd 1 (Right side): Ch 1, 8 sc in ring; join with
slip st to first sc, finish off.
Note: Mark Rnd 1 as **right** side.
Rnd 2: With **right** side facing, join Tan with slip st in
any sc; ch 1, 2 sc in same st and in each sc around;
join with slip st to first sc, finish off: 16 sc.
Rnd 3: With **right** side facing, join Rust with slip st
in any sc; (ch 3, 3 tr, ch 3, slip st) in same st, ch 4,
skip next 3 sc, ★ (slip st, ch 3, 3 tr, ch 3, slip st) in
next sc, ch 4, skip next 3 sc; repeat from ★ around;
join with slip st to first slip st, finish off: 4 ch-4 sps.
Rnd 4: With **right** side facing, join Green with slip st
in first tr of any 3-tr group; ch 1, 2 sc in same st,
(hdc, ch 2, hdc) in next tr, 2 sc in next tr, 5 dc in next
ch-4 sp, ★ 2 sc in next tr, (hdc, ch 2, hdc) in next tr,
2 sc in next tr, 5 dc in next ch-4 sp; repeat from
★ around; join with slip st to first sc: 44 sts and
4 ch-2 sps.
Rnd 5: Ch 1, sc in same st and in each st around,
working (sc, ch 2, sc) in each ch-2 sp; join with slip st
to first sc, finish off: 52 sc.

Rnd 6: With **right** side facing, join Rust with slip st
in any ch-2 sp; ch 2, (dc, ch 2, dc, hdc) in same sp,
★ † ch 1, (skip next sc, sc in next sc, ch 1) 6 times,
skip next sc †, (hdc, dc, ch 2, dc, hdc) in next ch-2 sp;
repeat from ★ 2 times **more**, then repeat from
† to † once; join with slip st to top of beginning ch-2,
finish off: 32 sps.
Rnd 7: With **right** side facing, join Ecru with slip st
in any ch-2 sp; ch 1, (sc, ch 2, sc) in same sp, ★ † sc
in next 2 sts, dc in sc one row **below** next ch-1 sp,
(dc in next sc, dc in sc one row **below** next ch-1 sp) 6
times, sc in next 2 sts †, (sc, ch 2, sc) in next ch-2 sp;
repeat from ★ 2 times **more**, then repeat from
† to † once; join with slip st to first sc, finish off:
76 sts and 4 ch-2 sps.
Rnd 8: With **right** side facing, join Tan with slip st in
any ch-2 sp; ch **3 (counts as first dc, now and
throughout)**, 2 dc in same sp, dc in each st around,
working 3 dc in each ch-2 sp; join with slip st to first
dc, finish off: 88 dc.
Rnd 9: With **right** side facing, join Green with slip st
in any dc; ch 3, dc in each dc around, working (2 dc,
ch 2, 2 dc) in center dc of each corner; join with
slip st to first dc: 100 dc.
Rnd 10: Ch 1, sc in each dc around, working 3 sc in
each ch-2 sp; join with slip st to first sc, finish off:
112 sc.

ASSEMBLY
With Green and working through **both** loops,
whipstitch Squares together, forming 6 vertical strips
of 8 Squares each *(Fig. 20b, page 142)*, beginning in
center sc of first corner and ending in center sc of
next corner; then whipstitch strips together.

EDGING
Rnd 1: With **right** side facing, join Rust with slip st
in any sc; ch 1, sc in each sc and in each joining
around, working 3 sc in center sc of each corner; join
with slip st to first sc, finish off.
Rnd 2: With **right** side facing, join Green with slip st
in any sc; ch 3, dc in each sc around, working 5 dc in
center sc of each corner; join with slip st to first dc,
finish off.
Rnd 3: With **right** side facing, join Tan with slip st in
any dc; ch 1, sc in each dc around, working 3 sc in
center dc of each corner; join with slip st to first sc,
finish off.

HARVEST APPEAL

Celebrating the fall harvest season, this exquisite afghan is an appealing accent in rust, green, and yellow. Flowing fringe — worked using long ends left while joining and finishing off — gives it a classic look.

Finished Size: 45" x 60"

MATERIALS
Worsted Weight Yarn:
Green - 20 ounces, (570 grams, 1,370 yards)
Rust - 10 ounces, (280 grams, 685 yards)
Yellow - 8 ounces, (230 grams, 550 yards)
Dk Rust - 6 ounces, (170 grams, 410 yards)
Crochet hook, size I (5.50 mm) **or** size needed for gauge

GAUGE: 14 dc and 8 rows = 4"

Gauge Swatch: $4^1/_4$"w x 4"h
Ch 17 **loosely**.
Work same as Afghan for 8 rows.
Finish off.

Note: Each row is worked across length of Afghan. When joining yarn and finishing off, leave an 8" length to be worked into fringe.

AFGHAN

With Green, ch 211 **loosely**.
Row 1 (Right side): Working in back ridges of beginning ch *(Fig. 2b, page 137)*, dc in fourth ch from hook **(3 skipped chs count as first dc)** and in each ch across: 209 dc.
Note: Mark Row 1 as **right** side.
Row 2: Ch 3 **(counts as first dc, now and throughout)**, turn; dc in next dc and in each dc across; finish off.
Row 3: With **right** side facing, join Yellow with slip st in first dc; ch 4 **(counts as first dc plus ch 1, now and throughout)**, skip next dc, dc in next dc, ★ ch 1, skip next dc, dc in next dc; repeat from ★ across; finish off: 105 dc and 104 ch-1 sps.
Row 4: With **wrong** side facing, join Rust with slip st in first dc; ch 3, dc in each ch-1 sp and in each dc across; finish off: 209 dc.
Row 5: With **right** side facing, join Dk Rust with slip st in first dc; ch 3, dc in next dc and in each dc across; finish off.

Row 6: With **wrong** side facing, join Rust with slip st in first dc; ch 3, dc in next dc and in each dc across; finish off.
Row 7: With **right** side facing, join Yellow with slip st in first dc; ch 4, skip next dc, dc in next dc, ★ ch 1, skip next dc, dc in next dc; repeat from ★ across; finish off: 105 dc and 104 ch-1 sps.
Row 8: With **wrong** side facing, join Green with slip st in first dc; ch 3, dc in each ch-1 sp and in each dc across; do **not** finish off: 209 dc.
Rows 9-11: Ch 3, turn; dc in next dc and in each dc across; at end of Row 11, finish off.
Row 12: With **wrong** side facing, join Yellow with slip st in first dc; ch 4, skip next dc, dc in next dc, ★ ch 1, skip next dc, dc in next dc; repeat from ★ across; finish off: 105 dc and 104 ch-1 sps.
Row 13: With **right** side facing, join Rust with slip st in first dc; ch 3, dc in each ch-1 sp and in each dc across; finish off: 209 dc.
Row 14: With **wrong** side facing, join Dk Rust with slip st in first dc; ch 3, dc in next dc and in each dc across; finish off.
Row 15: With **right** side facing, join Rust with slip st in first dc; ch 3, dc in next dc and in each dc across; finish off.
Row 16: With **wrong** side facing, join Yellow with slip st in first dc; ch 4, skip next dc, dc in next dc, ★ ch 1, skip next dc, dc in next dc; repeat from ★ across; finish off: 105 dc and 104 ch-1 sps.
Row 17: With **right** side facing, join Green with slip st in first dc; ch 3, dc in each ch-1 sp and in each dc across; do **not** finish off: 209 dc.
Rows 18-20: Ch 3, turn; dc in next dc and in each dc across; at end of Row 20, finish off.
Rows 21-90: Repeat Rows 3-20, 3 times; then repeat Rows 3-18 once **more**.
Finish off.

Holding a total of 10 strands of yarn together (3 strands each of Yellow and Green, and 2 strands each of Rust and Dk Rust), using photo as a guide for placement, add fringe across short edges of Afghan *(Figs. 22b & d, page 142)*.

RADIANT RIPPLES

*Bursting with the colors of the harvest, our toasty wrap will chase away autumn chills.
Closely worked cluster stitches create lots of rich texture in the rippled design.*

Finished Size: 48" x 64"

MATERIALS
Worsted Weight Yarn:
  Gold - 24 ounces, (680 grams, 1,580 yards)
  Maroon - 11 ounces, (310 grams, 725 yards)
  Green - 9 ounces, (260 grams, 595 yards)
Crochet hook, size I (5.50 mm) **or** size needed
  for gauge

GAUGE: 15 sts (point to point) and 5 rows = 4"

Gauge Swatch: 8"w x 4"h
Ch 35 **loosely**.
Work same as Afghan for 5 rows.
Finish off.

STITCH GUIDE

CLUSTER (uses next 5 sts)
★ YO, insert hook in **next** st, YO and pull up a
loop, YO and draw through 2 loops on hook;
repeat from ★ 4 times **more**, YO and draw
through all 6 loops on hook (*Figs. 12a & b,
page 139*).
END CLUSTER (uses last 3 sts)
★ YO, insert hook in **next** st, YO and pull up a
loop, YO and draw through 2 loops on hook;
repeat from ★ 2 times **more**, YO and draw
through all 4 loops on hook (*Figs. 12a & b,
page 139*).
BEGINNING CLUSTER (uses first 3 sts)
Ch 2, turn; ★ YO, insert hook in **next** st, YO and
pull up a loop, YO and draw through 2 loops on
hook; repeat from ★ once **more**, YO and draw
through all 3 loops on hook (*Figs. 12a & b,
page 139*).

AFGHAN
With MC, ch 195 **loosely**.

Row 1 (Right side)**:** YO, insert hook in fourth ch
from hook, YO and pull up a loop, YO and draw
through 2 loops on hook, YO, insert hook in next ch,
YO and pull up a loop, YO and draw through
2 loops on hook, YO and draw through all 3 loops
on hook, dc in next 5 chs, 4 dc in next ch, dc in next
5 chs, ★ work Cluster, dc in next 5 chs, 4 dc in next
ch, dc in next 5 chs; repeat from ★ across to last
3 chs, work End Cluster: 12 4-dc groups.
Note: Mark Row 1 as **right** side.
Row 2: Work Beginning Cluster, skip next 2 dc, 5 dc
in next dc, skip next 2 dc, 4 dc in sp **before** next dc
(*Fig. 18, page 141*), skip next 2 dc, 5 dc in next dc,
★ skip next 2 dc, work Cluster, skip next 2 dc, 5 dc
in next dc, skip next 2 dc, 4 dc in sp **before** next dc,
skip next 2 dc, 5 dc in next dc; repeat from ★ across
to last 5 sts, skip next 2 dc, work End Cluster
changing to Maroon (*Fig. 17a, page 141*): 13 Clusters.
Row 3: Work Beginning Cluster, skip next 2 dc, 5 dc
in next dc, skip next 2 dc, 4 dc in sp **before** next dc,
skip next 2 dc, 5 dc in next dc, ★ skip next 2 dc,
work Cluster, skip next 2 dc, 5 dc in next dc, skip
next 2 dc, 4 dc in sp **before** next dc, skip next 2 dc,
5 dc in next dc; repeat from ★ across to last 5 sts,
skip next 2 dc, work End Cluster.
Row 4: Work Beginning Cluster, skip next 2 dc, 5 dc
in next dc, skip next 2 dc, 4 dc in sp **before** next dc,
skip next 2 dc, 5 dc in next dc, ★ skip next 2 dc,
work Cluster, skip next 2 dc, 5 dc in next dc, skip
next 2 dc, 4 dc in sp **before** next dc, skip next 2 dc,
5 dc in next dc; repeat from ★ across to last 5 sts,
skip next 2 dc, work End Cluster changing to Gold.
Row 5: Work Beginning Cluster, skip next 2 dc, 5 dc
in next dc, skip next 2 dc, 4 dc in sp **before** next dc,
skip next 2 dc, 5 dc in next dc, ★ skip next 2 dc,
work Cluster, skip next 2 dc, 5 dc in next dc, skip
next 2 dc, 4 dc in sp **before** next dc, skip next 2 dc,
5 dc in next dc; repeat from ★ across to last 5 sts,
skip next 2 dc, work End Cluster.
Row 6: Work Beginning Cluster, skip next 2 dc, 5 dc
in next dc, skip next 2 dc, 4 dc in sp **before** next dc,
skip next 2 dc, 5 dc in next dc, ★ skip next 2 dc,
work Cluster, skip next 2 dc, 5 dc in next dc, skip
next 2 dc, 4 dc in sp **before** next dc, skip next 2 dc,
5 dc in next dc; repeat from ★ across to last 5 sts,
skip next 2 dc, work End Cluster changing to Green.
Rows 7 and 8: Repeat Rows 3 and 4.

Row 9: Work Beginning Cluster, skip next 2 dc, 5 dc in next dc, skip next 2 dc, 4 dc in sp **before** next dc, skip next 2 dc, 5 dc in next dc, ★ skip next 2 dc, work Cluster, skip next 2 dc, 5 dc in next dc, skip next 2 dc, 4 dc in sp **before** next dc, skip next 2 dc, 5 dc in next dc; repeat from ★ across to last 5 sts, skip next 2 dc, work End Cluster.

Row 10: Work Beginning Cluster, skip next 2 dc, 5 dc in next dc, skip next 2 dc, 4 dc in sp **before** next dc, skip next 2 dc, 5 dc in next dc, ★ skip next 2 dc, work Cluster, skip next 2 dc, 5 dc in next dc, skip next 2 dc, 4 dc in sp **before** next dc, skip next 2 dc, 5 dc in next dc; repeat from ★ across to last 5 sts, skip next 2 dc, work End Cluster changing to Maroon.

Repeat Rows 3-10 until Afghan measures approximately 63" from beginning ch, ending by working Row 5.

Last Row: Work Beginning Cluster, dc in next 5 dc, 4 dc in sp **before** next dc, dc in next 5 dc, ★ work Cluster, dc in next 5 dc, 4 dc in sp **before** next dc, dc in next 5 dc; repeat from ★ across to last 3 sts, work End Cluster; finish off.

Add Fringe in each point across short edges of afghan *(Figs. 22a & c, page 142)*.

91

LUXURIOUS WRAP

Shades of brown ripple with ecru to create the luxurious look of this wonderful autumn throw. Stitch it in the warm hues shown, or choose your own color combination for a personal touch.

Finished Size: 48$^1/_2$ " x 66$^1/_2$ "

MATERIALS
Worsted Weight Yarn:
Lt Brown - 22 ounces, (620 grams, 1,510 yards)
Brown - 17$^1/_2$ ounces, (500 grams, 1,200 yards)
Ecru - 12 ounces, (340 grams, 825 yards)
Crochet hook, size H (5.00 mm) **or** size needed for gauge

GAUGE: One repeat (point to point) = 3";
6 rows = 3$^1/_2$ "

Gauge Swatch: 6"w x 2$^3/_4$ "h
Ch 23 **loosely**.
Work same as Afghan Rows 1-4.
Finish off.

STITCH GUIDE

CLUSTER
★ YO, insert hook in st or sp indicated, YO and pull up a loop, YO and draw through 2 loops on hook; repeat from ★ 2 times **more**, YO and draw through all 4 loops on hook (*Figs. 11a & b, page 139*).
SINGLE CROCHET DECREASE
(abbreviated sc decrease)
Pull up a loop in next ch-1 sp and in last dc, YO and draw through all 3 loops on hook (**counts as one sc**).
DOUBLE CROCHET DECREASE
(abbreviated dc decrease)
YO, insert hook in next ch-1 sp, YO and pull up a loop, YO and draw through 2 loops on hook, YO, insert hook in last sc, YO and pull up a loop, YO and draw through 2 loops on hook, YO and draw through all 3 loops on hook (**counts as one dc**).

AFGHAN
With Brown, ch 177 **loosely**, place marker in second ch from hook for st placement.
Row 1 (Right side): Dc in fourth ch from hook, ch 1, skip next 2 chs, in next ch work [Cluster, ch 1, Cluster, ch 4, (Cluster, ch 1) twice], ★ skip next 2 chs, work Cluster in next ch, ch 1, skip next 4 chs, work Cluster in next ch, ch 1, skip next 2 chs, in next ch work [Cluster, ch 1, Cluster, ch 4, (Cluster, ch 1) twice]; repeat from ★ across to last 5 chs, skip next 2 chs, YO, insert hook in next ch, YO and pull up a loop, YO and draw through 2 loops on hook, YO, skip next ch, insert hook in last ch, YO and pull up a loop, YO and draw through 2 loops on hook, YO and draw through all 3 loops on hook; finish off: 94 Clusters and 95 sps.
Note: Mark Row 1 as **right** side.
Row 2: With **wrong** side facing, join Lt Brown with slip st in first st; ch 1, (sc in next ch-1 sp, ch 1) twice, (sc, ch 4, sc) in next ch-4 sp, ch 1, ★ (sc in next ch-1 sp, ch 1) 5 times, (sc, ch 4, sc) in next ch-4 sp, ch 1; repeat from ★ across to last 2 ch-1 sps, sc in next ch-1 sp, ch 1, sc decrease.
Row 3: Ch 2, turn; dc in first ch-1 sp, ch 1, skip next ch-1 sp, work [Cluster, ch 1, Cluster, ch 4, (Cluster, ch 1) twice] in next ch-4 sp, ★ skip next ch-1 sp, work Cluster in next ch-1 sp, ch 1, skip next 2 ch-1 sps, work Cluster in next ch-1 sp, ch 1, skip next ch-1 sp, work [Cluster, ch 1, Cluster, ch 4, (Cluster, ch 1) twice] in next ch-4 sp; repeat from ★ across to last 2 ch-1 sps, skip next ch-1 sp, dc decrease; finish off.
Row 4: With **wrong** side facing, join Ecru with slip st in first dc; ch 1, (sc in next ch-1 sp, ch 1) twice, (sc, ch 4, sc) in next ch-4 sp, ch 1, ★ (sc in next ch-1 sp, ch 1) 5 times, (sc, ch 4, sc) in next ch-4 sp, ch 1; repeat from ★ across to last 2 ch-1 sps, sc in next ch-1 sp, ch 1, sc decrease.
Row 5: Repeat Row 3.

Row 6: With **wrong** side facing, join Lt Brown with slip st in first dc; ch 1, (sc in next ch-1 sp, ch 1) twice, (sc, ch 4, sc) in next ch-4 sp, ch 1, ★ (sc in next ch-1 sp, ch 1) 5 times, (sc, ch 4, sc) in next ch-4 sp, ch 1; repeat from ★ across to last 2 ch-1 sps, sc in next ch-1 sp, ch 1, sc decrease.
Row 7: Repeat Row 3.
Row 8: With **wrong** side facing, join Brown with slip st in first dc; ch 1, (sc in next ch-1 sp, ch 1) twice, (sc, ch 4, sc) in next ch-4 sp, ch 1, ★ (sc in next ch-1 sp, ch 1) 5 times, (sc, ch 4, sc) in next ch-4 sp, ch 1; repeat from ★ across to last 2 ch-1 sps, sc in next ch-1 sp, ch 1, sc decrease.
Row 9: Repeat Row 3.
Row 10: With **wrong** side facing, join Lt Brown with slip st in first dc; ch 1, (sc in next ch-1 sp, ch 1) twice, (sc, ch 4, sc) in next ch-4 sp, ch 1, ★ (sc in next ch-1 sp, ch 1) 5 times, (sc, ch 4, sc) in next ch-4 sp, ch 1; repeat from ★ across to last 2 ch-1 sps, sc in next ch-1 sp, ch 1, sc decrease.
Rows 11-113: Repeat Rows 3-10, 12 times; then repeat Rows 3-9 once **more**.

Continued on page 94.

EDGING

With **right** side facing, join Brown with slip st in marked ch on Row 1; ch 1, sc evenly across end of rows; working in sts and in sps on Row 113, sc in first dc, ch 1, (sc in next ch-1 sp, ch 1) twice, (sc, ch 3, sc) in next ch-4 sp, ch 1, ★ (sc in next ch-1 sp, ch 1) 5 times, (sc, ch 3, sc) in next ch-4 sp, ch 1; repeat from ★ across to last 2 ch-1 sps, (sc in next ch-1 sp, ch 1) twice, sc in last dc; sc evenly across end of rows; working in sps and in free loops of beginning ch *(Fig. 15b, page 140)*, sc in first ch, ch 1, (sc in next sp, ch 1) twice, sc in ch at base of next 4-Cluster group, ch 1, † sc in next sp, ch 1, sc in ch at base of next Cluster, ch 1, (sc, ch 2, sc) in next sp, ch 1, sc in ch at base of next Cluster, ch 1, sc in next sp, ch 1, sc in ch at base of next 4-Cluster group, ch 1 †, repeat from † to † across to last 2 sps, (sc in next sp, ch 1) twice; join with slip st to first sc, finish off.

Holding 10 strands of Brown yarn together, add fringe in each point across short edges of Afghan *(Figs. 22a & c, page 142)*.

ABLAZE WITH COLOR

A great pattern for using up your scrap yarn, this afghan is ablaze with vibrant autumn color. Cluster stitches provide thick texture for the cuddly throw.

Finished Size: 52" x 62"

MATERIALS
Worsted Weight Yarn:
   Black - 38 ounces, (1,080 grams, 2,150 yards)
   Scraps - 32 ounces,
      (910 grams, 1,810 yards) **total**
      Note: Each Scrap row requires 31$^1/_2$ yards.
Crochet hook, size I (5.50 mm) **or** size needed
   for gauge

GAUGE: In pattern, (Cluster, ch 2, sc) twice = 3$^1/_4$";
      7 rows = 3$^3/_4$"

Gauge Swatch: 5"w x 3$^3/_4$"h
Ch 22 **loosely**.
Work same as Afghan for 7 rows.
Finish off.

STITCH GUIDE

CLUSTER (uses next 5 sts)
★ YO, insert hook in **next** st, YO and pull up a loop, YO and draw through 2 loops on hook; repeat from ★ 4 times **more**, YO and draw through all 6 loops on hook *(Figs. 12a & b, page 139)*.

AFGHAN
With Black, ch 196 **loosely**.
Row 1 (Right side): 2 Dc in fourth ch from hook **(3 skipped chs count as first dc)**, skip next 2 chs, sc in next ch, ★ skip next 2 chs, 5 dc in next ch, skip next 2 chs, sc in next ch; repeat from ★ across to last 3 chs, skip next 2 chs, 3 dc in last ch changing to Scrap color desired in last dc *(Fig. 17a, page 141)*: 161 dc and 32 sc.
Note: Mark Row 1 as **right** side.
Row 2: Ch 1, turn; sc in first dc, ★ ch 2, work Cluster, ch 2, sc in next dc; repeat from ★ across changing to Black in last sc: 32 Clusters and 33 sc.
Row 3: Ch 3 **(counts as first dc, now and throughout)**, turn; 2 dc in same st, sc in next Cluster, (5 dc in next sc, sc in next Cluster) across to last sc, 3 dc in last sc changing to next Scrap color desired in last dc: 161 dc and 32 sc.
Rows 4-115: Repeat Rows 2 and 3, 56 times; at end of Row 115, do **not** change colors, finish off.

Holding 10 strands of Black together, add fringe evenly spaced across short edges of Afghan *(Figs. 22a & c, page 142)*.

DIGNIFIED

On a background of variegated yarn, a contrasting color creates an eye-catching pattern on this extravagant afghan. Dignified edging adds a beautiful finish.

Finished Size: 49" x 68"

MATERIALS
Worsted Weight Yarn:
    Variegated - 42^1/$_2$ ounces,
      (1,210 grams, 2,465 yards)
    Teal - 15 ounces, (430 grams, 850 yards)
Crochet hook, size I (5.50 mm) **or** size needed
    for gauge
Safety pin
Yarn needle

GAUGE: Each Square = 4^3/$_4$ "

Gauge Swatch: 2^1/$_2$ " square
Work same as Square through Rnd 2.

STITCH GUIDE

> **ANCHOR DOUBLE CROCHET**
> *(abbreviated Anchor dc)*
> YO, insert hook in next dc **and** in back ridge of center ch of ch-5 *(Fig. 2b, page 137)*, YO and pull up a loop (3 loops on hook), (YO and draw through 2 loops on hook) twice.

SQUARE (Make 117)
Rnd 1 (Right side): With Variegated, ch 5, (dc, ch 1) 7 times in fifth ch from hook; join with slip st to fourth ch of beginning ch-5: 8 sts and 8 ch-1 sps.
Note: Mark Rnd 1 as **right** side.
Rnd 2: Ch 2 **(counts as first hdc)**, 2 hdc in same st, (dc, ch 1, tr, ch 1, dc) in next dc, ★ 3 hdc in next dc, (dc, ch 1, tr, ch 1, dc) in next dc; repeat from ★ 2 times **more**; join with slip st to first hdc, slip st in next hdc, place loop from hook onto safety pin to keep piece from unraveling as you work the next rnd: 24 sts and 8 ch-1 sps.
Rnd 3: With **wrong** side facing and holding safety pin and dropped yarn to **wrong** side, join Teal with sc in first ch **after** any corner tr *(see Joining With Sc, page 140)*; ★ † ch 1, skip next dc, (sc in next hdc, ch 1, skip next st) twice, sc in next ch, ch 3, skip next tr †, sc in next ch; repeat from ★ 2 times **more**, then repeat from † to † once; join with slip st to first sc, finish off: 16 sc and 16 sps.

Rnd 4: With **right** side facing and working **behind** Rnd 3, remove safety pin and place loop onto hook; ch 3 **(counts as first dc, now and throughout)**, sc in next sc on Rnd 3, ★ † working **behind** next ch-1 *(Fig. 16, page 141)*, dc in skipped dc on Rnd 2, ch 1, working in **front** of next corner ch-3, (dc, ch 1, tr, ch 1, dc) in skipped tr on Rnd 2, ch 1 †, (working **behind** next ch-1, dc in skipped st on Rnd 2, sc in next sc on Rnd 3) twice; repeat from ★ 2 times **more**, then repeat from † to † once, working **behind** next ch-1, dc in skipped dc on Rnd 2, sc in last sc on Rnd 3; join with slip st to first dc, slip st in next sc, place loop from hook onto safety pin to keep piece from unraveling as you work the next rnd: 32 sts and 16 ch-1 sps.
Rnd 5: With **wrong** side facing and holding safety pin and dropped yarn to **right** side, join Teal with sc in first ch **after** any corner tr; ★ † ch 1, working **behind** next ch-1, dc in skipped sc on Rnd 3, ch 5, skip next 5 sts on Rnd 4, working **behind** next ch-1, dc in skipped sc on Rnd 3, ch 1, skip next dc on Rnd 4, sc in next ch, ch 3, skip next tr †, sc in next ch; repeat from ★ 2 times **more**, then repeat from † to † once; join with slip st to first sc, finish off: 16 sts and 16 sps.
Rnd 6: With **right** side facing and working in **front** of Rnd 5, remove safety pin and place loop onto hook; ch 3, dc in next skipped dc on Rnd 4, ★ † sc in next dc on Rnd 5, working **behind** next ch-1, dc in skipped dc on Rnd 4, sc in next sc on Rnd 5, working **behind** next corner ch-3, (dc, ch 3, dc) in skipped tr on Rnd 4, sc in next sc on Rnd 5, working **behind** next ch-1, dc in skipped dc on Rnd 4, sc in next dc on Rnd 5, working in **front** of next ch-5, dc in next 2 skipped sts on Rnd 4, work Anchor dc †, working in **front** of same ch-5, dc in next 2 skipped sts on Rnd 4; repeat from ★ 2 times **more**, then repeat from † to † once; join with slip st to first dc, finish off: 52 sts and 4 ch-3 sps.

ASSEMBLY
With Variegated and working through **both** loops, whipstitch Squares together forming 9 vertical strips of 13 Squares each *(Fig. 20b, page 142)*, beginning in center ch of first corner ch-3 and ending in center ch of next corner ch-3; then whipstitch strips together in same manner.

Continued on page 98.

EDGING

Rnd 1: With **right** side facing, join Variegated with slip st in any corner ch-3 sp; ch 4, (tr, ch 1, 2 dc) in same sp, dc in next 13 sts, ★ (dc in next ch and in next joining, dc in next ch and in next 13 sts) across to next corner ch-3 sp, (2 dc, ch 1, tr, ch 1, 2 dc) in corner ch-3 sp, dc in next 13 sts; repeat from ★ 2 times **more**, (dc in next ch and in next joining, dc in next ch and in next 13 sts) across, dc in same sp as beginning ch-4; join with slip st to third ch of beginning ch-4, place loop from hook onto safety pin to keep piece from unraveling as you work the next rnd: 712 sts and 8 ch-1 sps.

Rnd 2: With **wrong** side facing and holding safety pin and dropped yarn to **wrong** side, join Teal with sc in first ch **after** any corner tr; ★ † ch 1, skip next dc, (sc in next st, ch 1, skip next dc) across to next ch, sc in ch, ch 3, skip next corner tr †, sc in next ch; repeat from ★ 2 times **more**, then repeat from † to † once; join with slip st to first sc, finish off: 360 sc and 360 sps.

Rnd 3: With **right** side facing and working **behind** Rnd 2, remove safety pin and place loop onto hook; ch 3, sc in next sc on Rnd 2, working **behind** next corner ch-3, (dc, ch 1, tr, ch 1, dc) in skipped tr on Rnd 1, sc in next sc on Rnd 2, ★ (working **behind** next ch-1, dc in skipped dc on Rnd 1, sc in next sc on Rnd 2) across to next corner ch-3, working **behind** corner ch-3, (dc, ch 1, tr, ch 1, dc) in skipped tr on Rnd 1, sc in next sc on Rnd 2; repeat from ★ 2 times **more**, (working **behind** next ch-1, dc in skipped dc on Rnd 1, sc in next sc on Rnd 2) across; join with slip st to first dc, place loop from hook onto safety pin to keep piece from unraveling as you work the next rnd: 728 sts and 8 ch-1 sps.

Rnd 4: Repeat Rnd 2: 368 sc and 368 sps.

Rnd 5: With **right** side facing and working **behind** Rnd 4, remove safety pin and place loop onto hook; ch 3, sc in next sc on Rnd 4, working in **front** of next ch-1, dc in skipped dc on Rnd 3, sc in next sc on Rnd 4, working **behind** next corner ch-3, (dc, ch 1, tr, ch 1, dc) in skipped tr on Rnd 3, sc in next sc on Rnd 4, working in **front** of next ch-1, dc in skipped dc on Rnd 3, sc in next sc on Rnd 4, ★ † working **behind** next ch-1, dc in skipped dc on Rnd 3, sc in next sc on Rnd 4, working in **front** of next ch-1, dc in skipped dc on Rnd 3, sc in next sc on Rnd 4 †, repeat from † to † across to next corner ch-3, working **behind** corner ch-3, (dc, ch 1, tr, ch 1, dc) in skipped tr on Rnd 3, sc in next sc on Rnd 4, working in **front** of next ch-1, dc in skipped dc on Rnd 3, sc in next sc on Rnd 4; repeat from ★ 2 times **more**, then repeat from † to † across; join with slip st to first dc, place loop from hook onto safety pin to keep piece from unraveling as you work the next rnd: 744 sts and 8 ch-1 sps.

Rnd 6: Repeat Rnd 2: 376 sc and 376 sps.

Rnd 7: With **right** side facing and working **behind** Rnd 6, remove safety pin and place loop onto hook; ch 3, sc in next sc on Rnd 6, working in **front** of next ch-1, dc in skipped dc on Rnd 5, sc in next sc on Rnd 6, working **behind** next ch-1, dc in skipped dc on Rnd 5, sc in next sc on Rnd 6, working **behind** next corner ch-3, (dc, ch 1, tr, ch 1, dc) in skipped tr on Rnd 5, sc in next sc on Rnd 6, ★ working **behind** next ch-1, dc in skipped dc on Rnd 5, sc in next sc on Rnd 6, † working in **front** of next ch-1, dc in skipped dc on Rnd 5, sc in next sc on Rnd 6, working **behind** next ch-1, dc in skipped dc on Rnd 5, sc in next sc on Rnd 6 †, repeat from † to † across to next corner ch-3, working **behind** corner ch-3, (dc, ch 1, tr, ch 1, dc) in skipped tr on Rnd 5, sc in next sc on Rnd 6; repeat from ★ 2 times **more**, (working **behind** next ch-1, dc in skipped dc on Rnd 5, sc in next sc on Rnd 6, working in **front** of next ch-1, dc in skipped dc on Rnd 5, sc in next sc on Rnd 6) across; join with slip st to first dc, place loop from hook onto safety pin to keep piece from unraveling as you work the next rnd: 760 sts and 8 ch-1 sps.

Rnd 8: Repeat Rnd 2: 384 sc and 384 sps.

Rnd 9: With **right** side facing and working **behind** Rnd 8, remove safety pin and place loop onto hook; ch 3, sc in next sc on Rnd 8, ★ (working **behind** next ch-1, dc in skipped dc on Rnd 7, sc in next sc on Rnd 8) across to next corner ch-3, working **behind** corner ch-3, (dc, ch 1, tr, ch 1, dc) in skipped tr on Rnd 7, sc in next sc on Rnd 8; repeat from ★ 3 times **more**, (working **behind** next ch-1, dc in skipped dc on Rnd 7, sc in next sc on Rnd 8) across; join with slip st to first dc: 776 sts and 8 ch-1 sps.

Rnd 10: Slip st in next sc, ch 1, sc in same st, ch 1, skip next dc, ★ (sc in next sc, ch 1, skip next dc) across to next ch-1 sp, sc in ch-1 sp, ch 3, skip next corner tr, sc in next ch-1 sp, ch 1, skip next dc; repeat from ★ 3 times **more**, (sc in next sc, ch 1, skip next dc) across; join with slip st to first sc.

Rnd 11: ★ (Slip st in next ch-1 sp, ch 1) across to next corner ch-3 sp, (slip st, ch 2, slip st) in corner ch-3 sp, ch 1; repeat from ★ 3 times **more**, (slip st in next ch-1 sp, ch 1) across; join with slip st to first slip st, finish off.

FOCAL POINT

If you're a "fan" of unique afghan designs, this gorgeous project is for you!
Rows of fans, framed by stripes, are the focal point of this decorator wrap.

Finished Size: 45" x 65"

MATERIALS
Worsted Weight Yarn:
    Black - 15 ounces, (430 grams, 850 yards)
    Green - 10 ounces, (280 grams, 565 yards)
    Tan - 10 ounces, (280 grams, 565 yards)
    Brown - 10 ounces, (280 grams, 565 yards)
Crochet hook, size I (5.50 mm) **or** size needed
    for gauge

GAUGE: In pattern, (sc, ch 1) 7 times = 3³/₄ ";
        8 rows = 3"

Gauge Swatch: 6"w x 3³/₄ "h
With Black, ch 22.
Work same as Afghan Body for 10 rows.
Finish off.

AFGHAN BODY
With Black, ch 162.
Row 1 (Right side)**:** Sc in second ch from hook,
★ ch 1, skip next ch, sc in next ch; repeat from ★
across: 81 sc and 80 ch-1 sps.
Note: Mark Row 1 as **right** side.

Row 2: Ch 1, turn; sc in first sc, (ch 1, sc in next sc) across; finish off.

Row 3: With **right** side facing, join Green with sc in first sc *(see Joining With Sc, page 140)*; ch 1, sc in next sc, ch 1, skip next ch-1 sp, (dc, ch 3, dc) in next ch-1 sp, ch 1, ★ skip next sc, (sc in next sc, ch 1) 3 times, skip next ch-1 sp, (dc, ch 3, dc) in next ch-1 sp, ch 1; repeat from ★ across to last 3 sc, skip next sc, sc in next sc, ch 1, sc in last sc: 16 ch-3 sps.

Row 4: Ch 1, turn; sc in first sc and in next ch-1 sp, ch 1, skip next sc, dc in next dc, 5 dc in next ch-3 sp, dc in next dc, ch 1, ★ skip next ch-1 sp, (sc in next ch-1 sp, ch 1) twice, skip next sc, dc in next dc, 5 dc in next ch-3 sp, dc in next dc, ch 1; repeat from ★ across to last 2 ch-1 sps, skip next ch-1 sp, sc in last ch-1 sp and in last sc: 112 dc and 47 ch-1 sps.

Row 5: Ch 1, turn; sc in first sc, skip next sc, sc in next dc, (ch 1, sc in next dc) 6 times, ★ skip next ch-1 sp, sc in next ch-1 sp, skip next sc, sc in next dc, (ch 1, sc in next dc) 6 times; repeat from ★ across to last 2 sc, skip next sc, sc in last sc; finish off: 129 sc.

Row 6: With **wrong** side facing, join Black with sc in first sc; sc in next sc, (ch 1, sc in next sc) 6 times, ★ working **behind** next sc *(Fig. 16, page 141)*, dc in skipped sc 2 rows **below**, skip sc in **front** of dc, sc in next sc, (ch 1, sc in next sc) 6 times; repeat from ★ across to last sc, sc in last sc; finish off.

Row 7: With **right** side facing, join Tan with slip st in first sc; ch 5 **(counts as first dtr)**, ★ skip next sc, dc in next sc, ch 1, hdc in next sc, ch 1, sc in next sc, ch 1, hdc in next sc, ch 1, dc in next sc, skip next sc, dtr in next st *(Fig. 8, page 138)*; repeat from ★ across: 97 sts and 64 ch-1 sps.

Row 8: Ch 1, turn; sc in first 2 sts, (ch 1, skip next ch-1 sp, sc in next st) 4 times, ★ ch 1, skip next dtr, sc in next dc, (ch 1, skip next ch-1 sp, sc in next st) 4 times; repeat from ★ across to last dtr, sc in last dtr; finish off: 82 sc and 79 ch-1 sps.

Row 9: With **right** side facing, join Black with sc in first sc; (sc in next sc, ch 1) across to last 2 sc, sc in last 2 sc; do **not** finish off.

Continued on page 100.

Row 10: Ch 1, turn; sc in first 2 sc, ch 1, (sc in next sc, ch 1) across to last 2 sc, sc in last 2 sc; finish off.

Row 11: With **right** side facing, join Brown with dc in first sc *(see Joining With Dc, page 140)*; ch 1, dc in same st, ch 1, skip next sc, (sc in next sc, ch 1) 3 times, ★ skip next ch-1 sp, (dc, ch 3, dc) in next ch-1 sp, ch 1, skip next sc, (sc in next sc, ch 1) 3 times; repeat from ★ across to last 2 sc, skip next sc, (dc, ch 1, dc) in last sc: 15 ch-3 sps.

Row 12: Ch **3 (counts as first dc)**, turn; 2 dc in next ch-1 sp, dc in next dc, ch 1, skip next ch-1 sp, (sc in next ch-1 sp, ch 1) twice, skip next sc, dc in next dc, ★ 5 dc in next ch-3 sp, dc in next dc, ch 1, skip next ch-1 sp, (sc in next ch-1 sp, ch 1) twice, skip next sc, dc in next dc; repeat from ★ across to last ch-1 sp, 2 dc in last ch-1 sp, dc in last dc: 113 dc and 48 ch-1 sps.

Row 13: Ch 1, turn; sc in first dc, (ch 1, sc in next dc) 3 times, skip next ch-1 sp, sc in next ch-1 sp, skip next sc, sc in next dc, ★ (ch 1, sc in next dc) 6 times, skip next ch-1 sp, sc in next ch-1 sp, skip next sc, sc in next dc; repeat from ★ across to last 3 dc, (ch 1, sc in next dc) 3 times; finish off: 129 sc.

Row 14: With **wrong** side facing, join Black with sc in first sc; (ch 1, sc in next sc) 3 times, working **behind** next sc, dc in skipped sc 2 rows **below**, skip sc in **front** of dc, sc in next sc, ★ (ch 1, sc in next sc) 6 times, working **behind** next sc, dc in skipped sc 2 rows **below**, skip sc in **front** of dc, sc in next sc; repeat from ★ across to last 3 sc, (ch 1, sc in next sc) 3 times; finish off.

Row 15: With **right** side facing, join Tan with sc in first sc; ★ ch 1, hdc in next sc, ch 1, dc in next sc, skip next sc, dtr in next dc, skip next sc, dc in next sc, ch 1, hdc in next sc, ch 1, sc in next sc; repeat from ★ across: 97 sts and 64 ch-1 sps.

Row 16: Ch 1, turn; sc in first sc, ch 1, (skip next ch-1 sp, sc in next st, ch 1) twice, skip next dtr, sc in next dc, ★ ch 1, (skip next ch-1 sp, sc in next st, ch 1) 4 times, skip next dtr, sc in next dc; repeat from ★ across to last 2 sts, (ch 1, skip next ch-1 sp, sc in next st) twice; finish off: 81 sc and 80 ch-1 sps.

Row 17: With **right** side facing, join Black with sc in first sc; (ch 1, sc in next sc) across.

Rows 18-170: Repeat Rows 2-17, 9 times; then repeat Rows 2-10 once **more**; at end of Row 170, do **not** finish off.

EDGING

Rnd 1: Ch 1, turn; sc in first sc, ch 1, [skip next sc, sc in top 2 loops of next ch *(Fig. 14, page 140)*, ch 1] across to last 2 sc, skip next sc, (sc, ch 2, sc) in last sc, ch 1; working in end of rows, skip next sc row, sc in next sc row, ch 1, sc in center of next dtr row, ch 1, sc in base of same row, ch 1, ★ (skip next 2 sc rows, sc in next sc row, ch 1, skip next sc row, sc in next sc row, ch 1) twice, skip next dc row, sc in top of next dc row, ch 1, sc in next sc row, ch 1, skip next sc row, sc in next sc row, ch 1, sc in center of next dtr row, ch 1, sc in base of same row, ch 1; repeat from ★ 9 times **more**, skip next 2 sc rows, sc in next sc row, ch 1, skip next sc row, sc in next sc row, ch 1, skip last row; working in free loops of beginning ch *(Fig. 15b, page 140)*, (sc, ch 2, sc) in first ch, ch 1, (skip next ch, sc in next ch, ch 1) across to last sp, skip next ch, (sc, ch 2, sc) in ch at base of last sc, ch 1; working in end of rows, skip first sc row, sc in next sc row, ch 1, skip next sc row, sc in next sc row, ch 1, skip next 2 sc rows, sc in base of next dtr row, ch 1, sc in center of same row, ch 1, sc in next sc row, ch 1, skip next sc row, sc in next sc row, † ch 1, sc in top of next dc row, ch 1, skip next dc row, (sc in next sc row, ch 1, skip next sc row, sc in next sc row, ch 1, skip next 2 sc rows) twice, sc in base of next dtr row, ch 1, sc in center of same row, ch 1, sc in next sc row, ch 1, skip next sc row, sc in next sc row †; repeat from † to † across, ch 2; join with slip st to first sc: 356 sps.

Rnd 2: Ch 1, do **not** turn; ★ (sc in next ch-1 sp, ch 1) across to next corner ch-2 sp, (sc, ch 2, sc) in corner ch-2 sp, ch 1; repeat from ★ around; join with slip st to first sc.

Rnd 3: ★ (Slip st in next ch-1 sp, ch 1) across to next corner ch-2 sp, (slip st, ch 2, slip st) in corner ch-2 sp, ch 1; repeat from ★ around to last ch-1 sp, slip st in last ch-1 sp, ch 1; join with slip st to first slip st, finish off.

CLASSIC ARAN

A wide variety of highly textured stitches is the key to this wrap's beauty.
Create the classic Aran-style afghan in any color to match your décor.

Finished Size: 48" x 66"

MATERIALS
Worsted Weight Yarn:
   57 ounces, (1,620 grams, 3,910 yards)
Crochet hook, size K (6.50 mm) **or** size needed
   for gauge
Yarn needle

GAUGE: Panel A = 12" wide; 10 rows = $4^1/_2$ "
   Panel B = $5^1/_2$ " wide; 6 rows = $3^3/_4$ "

Gauge Swatch: $4^3/_4$ "w x $4^1/_4$ "h
Ch 16 **loosely**.
Work same as Panel A, page 103, for 9 rows.
Finish off.

STITCH GUIDE

LOCKED TREBLE CROCHET
   (abbreviated Locked tr)
YO twice, insert hook from **front** to **back** in st
indicated and from **back** to **front** in next st, YO
and pull up a loop (4 loops on hook), (YO and
draw through 2 loops on hook) 3 times.

LOCKED CLUSTER
First Leg: YO twice, insert hook from **front** to
back in st indicated and from **back** to **front** in
next st, YO and pull up a loop (4 loops on hook),
(YO and draw through 2 loops on hook) twice
(2 loops remaining on hook).
Second Leg: YO twice, skip next Ch Loop and
next sc one row **below**, insert hook from **front** to
back in next st and from **back** to **front** in next st,
YO and pull up a loop, (YO and draw through
2 loops on hook) twice, YO and draw through all
3 loops on hook.

CHAIN LOOP *(abbreviated Ch Loop)*
Insert hook in st indicated, YO and pull up a
loop, (YO and draw through one loop on
hook) 3 times, YO and draw through both loops
on hook. Push Ch Loop to **right** side.

FRONT POST TREBLE CROCHET
   (abbreviated FPtr)
YO twice, insert hook from **front** to **back** around
post of st indicated *(Fig. 10, page 139)*, YO and
pull up a loop (4 loops on hook), (YO and draw
through 2 loops on hook) 3 times. Skip st behind
FPtr.

BACK POST TREBLE CROCHET
   (abbreviated BPtr)
YO twice, insert hook from **back** to **front** around
post of st indicated *(Fig. 10, page 139)*, YO and
pull up a loop (4 loops on hook), (YO and draw
through 2 loops on hook) 3 times. Skip st behind
BPtr.

LEFT FRONT POST CLUSTER
   (abbreviated Left FP Cluster)
First Leg: YO twice, insert hook from **front** to
back around post of st indicated *(Fig. 10,
page 139)*, YO and pull up a loop, (YO and draw
through 2 loops on hook) twice (2 loops
remaining on hook).
Second Leg: YO, insert hook in next st, YO and
pull up a loop, YO and draw through 2 loops on
hook, YO and draw through all 3 loops on hook.

LEFT BACK POST CLUSTER
   (abbreviated Left BP Cluster)
First Leg: YO twice, insert hook from **back** to
front around post of st indicated *(Fig. 10,
page 139)*, YO and pull up a loop, (YO and draw
through 2 loops on hook) twice (2 loops
remaining on hook).
Second Leg: YO, insert hook in next st, YO and
pull up a loop, YO and draw through 2 loops on
hook, YO and draw through all 3 loops on hook.

RIGHT FRONT POST CLUSTER
   (abbreviated Right FP Cluster)
First Leg: YO, insert hook in st indicated, YO
and pull up a loop, YO and draw through
2 loops on hook (2 loops remaining on hook).
Second Leg: YO twice, insert hook from **front** to
back around post of st indicated *(Fig. 10,
page 139)*, YO and pull up a loop, (YO and draw
through 2 loops on hook) twice, YO and draw
through all 3 loops on hook.

RIGHT BACK POST CLUSTER
(abbreviated Right BP Cluster)

First Leg: YO, insert hook in st indicated, YO and pull up a loop, YO and draw through 2 loops on hook (2 loops remaining on hook).
Second Leg: YO twice, insert hook from **back** to **front** around post of st indicated *(Fig. 10, page 139)*, YO and pull up a loop, (YO and draw through 2 loops on hook) twice, YO and draw through all 3 loops on hook.

CLUSTER

YO twice, insert hook from **front** to **back** around post st portion of same st as Second Leg of last Left FP Cluster made *(Fig. 10, page 139)*, YO and pull up a loop, (YO and draw through 2 loops on hook) twice (2 loops on hook), YO, insert hook in next dc, YO and pull up a loop, YO and draw through 2 loops on hook (3 loops on hook), YO twice, insert hook from **front** to **back** around post st portion of next Left BP Cluster, YO and pull up a loop, (YO and draw through 2 loops on hook) twice, YO and draw through all 4 loops on hook.

PUFF STITCH *(abbreviated Puff St)*
YO, insert hook in next dc, YO and pull up a loop even with loops on hook, ★ YO, insert hook in **same** st, YO and pull up a loop even with loops on hook; repeat from ★ 3 times **more**, YO and draw through all 11 loops on hook *(Fig. 13, page 139)*.

PANEL A (Make 3)

Ch 40 **loosely**.

Row 1 (Right side): Sc in second ch from hook and in next 2 chs, (work Ch Loop in next ch, sc in next 3 chs) across: 39 sts.
Note: Mark Row 1 as **right** side and bottom edge.
Row 2: Ch 3 **(counts as first dc, now and throughout)**, turn; dc in next sc and in each st across: 39 dc.
Row 3: Ch 1, turn; sc in first dc, work Ch Loop in next dc, sc in next dc, skip first sc on Row 1, work First Leg of Locked Cluster in next sc, work Second Leg of Locked Cluster, skip next dc from last sc made, sc in next dc, work Ch Loop in next dc, sc in next dc, ★ working **above** Second Leg of last Locked Cluster made, work First Leg of Locked Cluster in same st, work Second Leg of Locked Cluster, skip next dc from last sc made, sc in next dc, work Ch Loop in next dc, sc in next dc; repeat from ★ across: 9 Locked Clusters.
Row 4: Ch 3, turn; dc in next st and in each st across.

Row 5: Ch 1, turn; sc in first dc, work Locked tr in first Locked Cluster one row **below**, skip next dc from last sc made, sc in next dc, work Ch Loop in next dc, sc in next dc, working **above** Locked tr, work First Leg of Locked Cluster in same st as last Locked tr made, work Second Leg of Locked Cluster, skip next dc from last sc made, sc in next dc, work Ch Loop in next dc, sc in next dc, ★ working **above** Second Leg of last Locked Cluster made, work First Leg of Locked Cluster in same st, work Second Leg of Locked Cluster, skip next dc from last sc made, sc in next dc, work Ch Loop in next dc, sc in next dc; repeat from ★ across to last 2 dc, working **above** Second Leg of last Locked Cluster made, work Locked tr in same st, skip next dc from last sc made, sc in last dc.
Row 6: Ch 3, turn; dc in next st and in each st across.
Row 7: Ch 1, turn; sc in first dc, work Ch Loop in next dc, sc in next dc, work First Leg of Locked Cluster in Locked tr one row **below**, work Second Leg of Locked Cluster, skip next dc from last sc made, sc in next dc, work Ch Loop in next dc, sc in next dc, ★ working **above** Second Leg of last Locked Cluster made, work First Leg of Locked Cluster in same st, work Second Leg of Locked Cluster, skip next dc from last sc made, sc in next dc, work Ch Loop in next dc, sc in next dc; repeat from ★ across.
Rows 8-143: Repeat Rows 4-7, 34 times.
Finish off.

PANEL B (Make 2)

Ch 20 **loosely**.

Row 1: Dc in fourth ch from hook **(3 skipped chs count as first dc)** and in each ch across: 18 dc.
Row 2 (Right side): Ch 3 **(counts as first dc, now and throughout)**, turn; work FPtr around next dc, dc in next dc, work FPtr around next dc, dc in next 2 dc, work First Leg of Right FP Cluster in next dc, work Second Leg of Right FP Cluster around next dc, work First Leg of Right FP Cluster in same st as Second Leg of last Right FP Cluster made, work Second Leg of Right FP Cluster around next dc, skip dc behind Second Leg of Right FP Cluster just made, dc in next dc, ★ work First Leg of Left FP Cluster around post of same dc as last st made, work Second Leg of Left FP Cluster; repeat from ★ once **more**, dc in next 2 dc, (work FPtr around next dc, dc in next dc) twice: 17 sts.
Note: Mark Row 2 as **right** side and bottom edge.

Continued on page 104.

Row 3: Ch 3, turn; (work BPtr around next FPtr, dc in next dc) twice, work First Leg of Right BP Cluster in next dc, work Second Leg of Right BP Cluster around post st portion of next Left FP Cluster, work First Leg of Right BP Cluster in same st as Second Leg of last Right BP Cluster made, work Second Leg of Right BP Cluster around post st portion of next Left FP Cluster, dc in same st as Second Leg of last Right BP Cluster made and in next 2 sts, ★ work First Leg of Left BP Cluster around post st portion of Right FP Cluster just worked into, work Second Leg of Left BP Cluster; repeat from ★ once **more**, dc in next dc, (work BPtr around next FPtr, dc in next dc) twice.

Row 4: Ch 3, turn; (work FPtr around next BPtr, dc in next dc) twice, (work FPtr around post st portion of next Left BP Cluster) twice, dc in next dc, work Puff St, dc in next dc, (work FPtr around post st portion of next Right BP Cluster) twice, dc in next dc, (work FPtr around next BPtr, dc in next dc) twice.

Row 5: Ch 3, turn; work BPtr around next FPtr, dc in next dc, work BPtr around next FPtr, dc in next 2 sts, ★ work First Leg of Left BP Cluster around same st as last st made, work Second Leg of Left BP Cluster; repeat from ★ once **more**, dc in next Puff St, work First Leg of Right BP Cluster in next dc, work Second Leg of Right BP Cluster around next FPtr, work First Leg of Right BP Cluster in same st as Second Leg of last Right BP Cluster made, work Second Leg of Right BP Cluster around next FPtr, dc in same st as Second Leg of last Right BP Cluster made and in next dc, (work BPtr around next FPtr, dc in next dc) twice.

Row 6: Ch 3, turn; work FPtr around next BPtr, dc in next dc, work FPtr around next BPtr, dc in next 3 sts, work First Leg of Left FP Cluster around post st portion of Right BP Cluster just worked into, work Second Leg of Left FP Cluster, work Cluster, work First Leg of Right FP Cluster in same st as third leg of last Cluster made, work Second Leg of Right FP Cluster around post st portion of next Left BP Cluster, dc in same st as Second Leg of last Right FP Cluster made and in next 2 dc, (work FPtr around next BPtr, dc in next dc) twice.

Row 7: Ch 3, turn; work BPtr around next FPtr, dc in next dc, work BPtr around next FPtr, dc in next 4 sts, 2 dc in next Cluster, dc in next 4 sts, (work BPtr around next FPtr, dc in next dc) twice: 18 sts.

Row 8: Ch 3, turn; work FPtr around next BPtr, dc in next dc, work FPtr around next BPtr, dc in next 2 dc, work First Leg of Right FP Cluster in next dc, work Second Leg of Right FP Cluster around next dc, work First Leg of Right FP Cluster in same st as Second Leg of last Right FP Cluster made, work Second Leg of Right FP Cluster around next dc, skip dc behind Second Leg of last Right FP Cluster made, dc in next dc, ★ work First Leg of Left FP Cluster around same dc as last st made, work Second Leg of Left FP Cluster; repeat from ★ once **more**, dc in next 2 dc, (work FPtr around next BPtr, dc in next dc) twice: 17 sts.

Rows 9-103: Repeat Rows 3-8, 15 times; then repeat Rows 3-7 once **more**.
Finish off.

ASSEMBLY

Afghan is assembled by joining Panels in the following sequence: Panel A, (Panel B, Panel A) twice.

With **right** side of two Panels facing you, bottom edges at same end and edges even, sew through both pieces once to secure the beginning of the seam, leaving an ample yarn end to weave in later. Insert the needle from **right** to **left** through one strand on each piece *(Fig. 21, page 142)*. Bring the needle around and insert it from **right** to **left** through the next strand on both pieces. Continue in this manner, drawing seam together as you work.

EDGING

Rnd 1: With **right** side facing, join yarn with slip st in first sc on Row 143 in top right corner; ch 3, dc in same st, working across top of each Panel, dc in each st across to last sc on last Panel A, 3 dc in last sc; working across end of rows, skip first sc row, (2 dc in next dc row, dc in next sc row) across; working in free loops of beginning chs on each Panel *(Fig. 15b, page 140)*, 3 dc in first ch, dc in each ch across to ch at base of last sc on last Panel A, 3 dc in last ch; working across end of rows, dc in first sc row, 2 dc in next dc row, (dc in next sc row, 2 dc in next dc row) across to last sc row, skip last sc row, dc in same st as first dc; join with slip st to first dc: 740 dc.

Rnd 2: Ch 1, work (Ch Loop, sc, Ch Loop) in same st, sc in next dc, ★ (work Ch Loop in next dc, sc in next dc) across to center dc of next corner 3-dc group, work (Ch Loop, sc, Ch Loop) in center dc, sc in next dc; repeat from ★ 2 times **more**, (work Ch Loop in next dc, sc in next dc) across; join with slip st to first st, finish off.

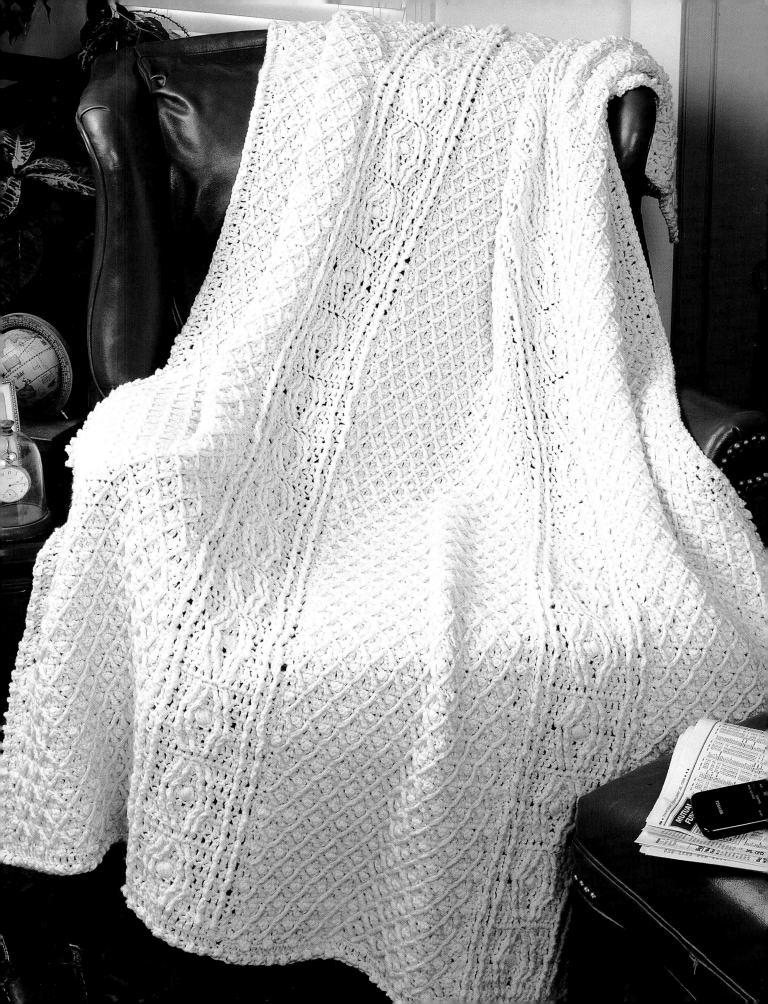

WINTER

*Snow is falling outside and there's a blazing fire in the hearth —
what better time than this to cuddle up with a cozy throw from our
beautiful winter collection! This vibrant assortment of classic
designs and hearty textures offers something for everyone
on your gift list, just in time for the holiday season.*

FROSTY WINDOWS

Although its blocks resemble frosty windowpanes, this afghan will keep you safe from winter's chill. Puff stitches form the focal point of each mesh-work square.

Finished Size: 49" x 67"

MATERIALS
Worsted Weight Yarn:
   41 ounces, (1,170 grams, 2,695 yards)
Crochet hook, size H (5.00 mm) **or** size needed
   for gauge
Yarn needle

GAUGE: Each Square = 6"

STITCH GUIDE

PUFF STITCH *(abbreviated Puff St)*
★ YO, insert hook in sp indicated, YO and pull up a ¹/₂" loop; repeat from ★ 2 times **more**, YO and draw through all 7 loops on hook *(Fig. 1)*.

Fig. 1

SQUARE (Make 88)
Ch 4; join with slip st to form a ring.
Rnd 1 (Right side): Ch 3, 11 dc in ring; join with slip st to top of beginning ch-3: 12 sts.
Note: Mark Rnd 1 as **right** side.
Rnd 2: Slip st in sp **before** next dc *(Fig. 18, page 141)*, work Puff St in same sp, (ch 1, skip next dc, work Puff St in sp **before** next dc) twice, ch 5 (corner), skip next dc, ★ work Puff St in sp **before** next dc, (ch 1, skip next dc, work Puff St in sp **before** next dc) twice, ch 5, skip next dc; repeat from ★ around; join with slip st to top of first Puff St: 12 Puff Sts.
Rnd 3: Slip st in next ch-1 sp, work Puff St in same sp, ch 1, work Puff St in next ch-1 sp, ch 2, 5 dc in next corner loop, ch 2, ★ work Puff St in next ch-1 sp, ch 1, work Puff St in next ch-1 sp, ch 2, 5 dc in next corner loop, ch 2; repeat from ★ around; join with slip st to top of first Puff St.

Rnd 4: Slip st in next ch-1 sp, work Puff St in same sp, ch 2, skip next ch-2 sp, (dc in next dc, ch 1) twice, (dc, ch 1) 3 times in next corner dc, dc in next dc, ch 1, dc in next dc, ★ ch 2, skip next ch-2 sp, work Puff St in next ch-1 sp, ch 2, skip next ch-2 sp, (dc in next dc, ch 1) twice, (dc, ch 1) 3 times in next corner dc, dc in next dc, ch 1, dc in next dc; repeat from ★ around, ch 1, skip last ch-2 sp, sc in top of first Puff St to form last sp.
Rnd 5: Ch 4, dc in next ch-2 sp, ch 1, (dc in next dc, ch 1) 3 times, (dc, ch 1) 3 times in next corner dc, (dc in next dc, ch 1) 3 times, ★ (dc in next ch-2 sp, ch 1) twice, (dc in next dc, ch 1) 3 times, (dc, ch 1) 3 times in next corner dc, (dc in next dc, ch 1) 3 times; repeat from ★ around; join with slip st to third ch of beginning ch-4: 44 ch-1 sps.
Rnd 6: Ch 4, (dc in next dc, ch 1) 5 times, (dc, ch 1) 3 times in next corner dc, ★ (dc in next dc, ch 1) 10 times, (dc, ch 1) 3 times in next corner dc; repeat from ★ 2 times **more**, (dc in next dc, ch 1) 4 times; join with slip st to third ch of beginning ch-4, finish off.

JOINING
Working through **both** loops, whipstitch Squares together, forming 8 vertical strips of 11 Squares each *(Fig. 20b, page 142)*; then whipstitch strips together.

EDGING
Rnd 1: With **right** side facing, join yarn with slip st in any corner dc; ★ (work Puff St, ch 2) twice in corner dc, (work Puff St in next dc, ch 2) 12 times, † work Puff St in joining, ch 2, (work Puff St in next dc, ch 2) 12 times †, repeat from † to † across to next corner dc; repeat from ★ around; join with slip st to top of first Puff St.
Rnd 2: Ch 3, dc in same st, slip st in next ch-2 sp, 2 dc in next Puff St, slip st in next ch-2 sp, (dc in next Puff St, slip st in next ch-2 sp) across to first corner Puff St, ★ 2 dc in Puff St, slip st in next ch-2 sp, 2 dc in next Puff St, slip st in next ch-2 sp, (dc in next Puff St, slip st in next ch-2 sp) across to first corner Puff St; repeat from ★ around; join with slip st to top of beginning ch-3, finish off.

COZY CHECKS

You'll definitely want to "check out" this striking wrap! Crocheted in black and jewel tones, it's an eye-catching companion for gray winter days.

Finished Size: 48" x 62"

MATERIALS
Worsted Weight Yarn:
Black - $29^1/2$ ounces, (840 grams, 1,665 yards)
Green - $9^1/2$ ounces, (270 grams, 535 yards)
Rose - $9^1/2$ ounces, (270 grams, 535 yards)
Blue - $8^1/2$ ounces, (240 grams, 480 yards)
Crochet hook, size H (5.00 mm) **or** size needed for gauge

GAUGE: In pattern, 14 dc = 4"; 11 rows = $3^3/4$"

Gauge Swatch: 5" square
With Black, ch 19 **loosely**.
Work same as Afghan Body for 15 rows.

AFGHAN BODY

With Black, ch 157 **loosely**, place marker in third ch from hook for st placement.
Row 1 (Wrong side): Dc in fourth ch from hook **(3 skipped chs count as first dc)** and in each ch across; finish off: 155 dc.
Note: Mark the **back** of any stitch on Row 1 as **right** side.
Row 2: With **right** side facing, join Green with slip st in first dc; ch 3 **(counts as first dc)**, dc in next 3 dc, ch 3, ★ skip next 3 dc, dc in next 3 dc, ch 3; repeat from ★ across to last 7 dc, skip next 3 dc, dc in last 4 dc; finish off: 80 dc and 25 ch-3 sps.
Row 3: With **wrong** side facing, join Black with slip st in first dc; ch 5 **(counts as first hdc plus ch 3)**, ★ skip next 3 dc, working **around** next ch-3, dc in next 3 dc one row **below** ch-3, ch 3; repeat from ★ across to last 4 dc, skip next 3 dc, hdc in last dc; finish off: 77 sts and 26 ch-3 sps.
Row 4: With **right** side facing, join Blue with slip st in first hdc; ch 2 **(counts as first hdc, now and throughout)**, working **around** next ch-3, dc in next 3 dc one row **below** ch-3, ★ ch 3, skip next 3 dc, working **around** next ch-3, dc in next 3 dc one row **below** ch-3; repeat from ★ across to last hdc, hdc in last hdc; finish off: 80 sts and 25 ch-3 sps.

Row 5: Repeat Row 3.
Row 6: With Rose, repeat Row 4.
Row 7: Repeat Row 3.
Row 8: With Green, repeat Row 4.
Rows 9-170: Repeat Rows 3-8, 27 times.
Row 171: With **wrong** side facing, join Black with slip st in first hdc; ch 2, ★ hdc in next 3 dc, working **around** next ch-3, dc in next 3 dc one row **below** ch-3; repeat from ★ across to last 4 sts, hdc in last 4 sts; do **not** finish off: 155 sts.

EDGING

Rnd 1: Ch 1, turn; sc in first hdc and in each st across to last hdc, 3 sc in last hdc; sc evenly across end of rows; working in free loops of beginning ch *(Fig. 15b, page 140)*, 3 sc in marked ch, sc in each ch across to last ch, 3 sc in last ch; sc evenly across end of rows; 2 sc in same st as first sc; join with slip st to first sc.
Rnd 2: Ch 1, do **not** turn; sc in same st and in each sc around working 3 sc in center sc of each corner 3-sc group; join with slip st to first sc, finish off.
Rnd 3: With **right** side facing, join Green with sc in center sc of any corner 3-sc group *(see Joining With Sc, page 140)*; 2 sc in same st, sc in each sc around working 3 sc in center sc of each corner 3-sc group; join with slip st to first sc, finish off.
Rnd 4: With **right** side facing, join Black with sc in center sc of any corner 3-sc group; 2 sc in same st, sc in each sc around working 3 sc in center sc of each corner 3-sc group; join with slip st to first sc, finish off.
Rnd 5: With Rose, repeat Rnd 4.
Rnd 6: Repeat Rnd 4; do **not** finish off.
Rnd 7: Ch 1, sc in same st and in each sc around working 3 sc in center sc of each corner 3-sc group; join with slip st to first sc, finish off.

WINTER ABLOOM

*Golden-throated poinsettia motifs shine against a background of dark green
on our toasty afghan. What a festive way to decorate for winter!*

Finished Size: 50" x 71"

MATERIALS
Worsted Weight Yarn:
Green - 54 ounces, (1,530 grams, 3,705 yards)
Gold - 4¹/₂ ounces, (130 grams, 310 yards)
Red - 7 ounces, (200 grams, 480 yards)
Crochet hook, size G (4.00 mm) **or** size needed
for gauge
Yarn needle

GAUGE: Each Square = 7"

STITCH GUIDE

BEGINNING CLUSTER
Ch 2, ★ YO, insert hook in sp indicated, YO and
pull up a loop, YO and draw through 2 loops on
hook; repeat from ★ once **more**, YO and draw
through all 3 loops on hook *(Figs. 11a & b,
page 139)*.
CLUSTER
★ YO, insert hook in sp indicated, YO and pull
up a loop, YO and draw through 2 loops on
hook; repeat from ★ 2 times **more**, YO and draw
through all 4 loops on hook *(Figs. 11a & b,
page 139)*.

SQUARE (Make 70)
With Gold, ch 6; join with slip st to form a ring.
Rnd 1 (Right side): Work beginning Cluster in ring,
ch 3, (work Cluster in ring, ch 3) 7 times; join with
slip st to top of beginning Cluster, finish off:
8 Clusters.
Note: Mark Rnd 1 as **right** side.
Rnd 2: With **right** side facing, join Red with slip st in
any ch-3 sp; work (beginning Cluster, ch 3, Cluster)
in same sp, ch 3, (work Cluster, ch 3) twice in each
ch-3 sp around; join with slip st to top of beginning
Cluster, finish off: 16 Clusters.

Rnd 3: With **right** side facing, join Green with slip st
in first ch-3 sp; ch 3 **(counts as first dc, now and
throughout)**, (2 dc, ch 3, 3 dc) in same sp, ch 1, skip
next ch-3 sp, 3 dc in next ch-3 sp, ch 1, skip next
ch-3 sp, ★ (3 dc, ch 3, 3 dc) in next ch-3 sp, ch 1, skip
next ch-3 sp, 3 dc in next ch-3 sp, ch 1, skip next
ch-3 sp; repeat from ★ around; join with slip st to
first dc: 12 sps.
Rnds 4-7: Slip st in next 2 dc and in next ch-3 sp,
ch 3, (2 dc, ch 3, 3 dc) in same sp, ch 1, (3 dc in next
ch-1 sp, ch 1) across to next ch-3 sp, ★ (3 dc, ch 3,
3 dc) in ch-3 sp, ch 1, (3 dc in next ch-1 sp, ch 1)
across to next ch-3 sp; repeat from ★ around; join
with slip st to first dc: 28 sps.
Finish off.

ASSEMBLY
With Green and working through **both** loops of each
stitch on **both** pieces, whipstitch Squares together
forming 7 vertical strips of 10 Squares each *(Fig. 20b,
page 142)*, beginning in center ch of first corner and
ending in center ch of next corner; then whipstitch
strips together.

EDGING
With **right** side facing, join Green with slip st in any
corner ch-3 sp; ch 3, (2 dc, ch 3, 3 dc) in same sp,
ch 1, ★ † (3 dc in next ch-1 sp, ch 1) 6 times, [dc in
next sp, dc in next joining and in next sp, ch 1, (3 dc
in next ch-1 sp, ch 1) 6 times] across to next corner
ch-3 sp †, (3 dc, ch 3, 3 dc) in ch-3 sp, ch 1; repeat
from ★ 2 times **more**, then repeat from † to † once;
join with slip st to first dc, finish off.

With Green, add fringe across short edges of Afghan
(Figs. 22a & c, page 142).

SKI LODGE

Inspired by a colorful ski sweater, this throw is a delightful addition to your rustic décor. A simple edging adds to its classic look.

Finished Size: 51" x 69"

MATERIALS

Worsted Weight Yarn:
   White - 33 ounces, (940 grams, 2,080 yards)
   Black - 25 ounces, (710 grams, 1,575 yards)
   Red - $4^1/_2$ ounces, (120 grams, 280 yards)
   Green - $4^1/_2$ ounces, (120 grams, 280 yards)
Crochet hook, size I (5.50 mm) **or** size needed for gauge
Yarn needle

GAUGE: 14 sc and 16 rows = 4"

STRIP (Make 10)

Note: Strip will measure approximately $6^3/_4$" x 50".

FIRST SIDE

With Green, ch 176 **loosely**.
Row 1 (Right side): Sc in second ch from hook, (ch 1, skip next ch, sc in next ch) across changing to Red in last sc *(Fig. 17a, page 141)*: 88 sc.
Note: Mark Row 1 as **right** side.
Row 2: Ch 1, turn; sc in first sc, (ch 1, sc in next sc) across changing to Black in last sc.
Row 3: Ch 1, turn; sc in first sc, working in **front** of next ch-1 *(Fig. 16, page 141)*, dc in ch-1 sp one row **below** ch-1, sc in next sc, ★ working **behind** next ch-1, dc in ch-1 sp one row **below** ch-1, sc in next sc, working in **front** of next ch-1, dc in ch-1 sp one row **below** ch-1, sc in next sc; repeat from ★ across, do **not** change color: 175 sts.
Row 4: Ch 1, turn; sc in first sc, (ch 1, skip next dc, sc in next sc) across changing to White in last sc: 88 sc.
Row 5: Ch 1, turn; sc in first sc, working in **front** of next ch-1, dc in dc one row **below** ch 1, sc in next sc, working **behind** next ch-1, dc in dc one row **below** ch-1, sc in next sc, ★ (working in **front** of next ch-1, dc in dc one row **below** ch-1, sc in next sc) 3 times, working **behind** next ch-1, dc in dc one row **below** ch-1, sc in next sc; repeat from ★ across to last ch-1, working in **front** of last ch-1, dc in dc one row **below** ch-1, sc in last sc changing to Black: 175 sts.

Row 6: Ch 1, turn; sc in first sc, ch 1, skip next dc, sc in next sc, ch 1, skip next dc, working **behind** skipped dc, slip st in ch-1 sp one row **below** skipped dc, ch 2, sc in next sc, ★ (ch 2, skip next 2 sts, sc in next st) twice, ch 1, skip next dc, working **behind** skipped dc, slip st in ch-1 sp one row **below** skipped dc, ch 2, sc in next sc; repeat from ★ across to last 2 sts, ch 1, skip next dc, sc in last sc changing to White: 67 sc.
Row 7: Ch 1, turn; sc in first sc, working in **front** of next ch-1, dc in dc one row **below** ch-1, sc in next sc, dc in skipped dc one row **below**, sc in next sc, ★ [working in **front** of next ch-2, (dc in **next** st one row **below** ch-2) twice, sc in next sc] 2 times, dc in skipped dc one row **below**, sc in next sc; repeat from ★ across to last ch-1, working in **front** of last ch-1, dc in dc one row **below** ch-1, sc in last sc changing to Black: 175 sts.
Row 8: Ch 1, turn; sc in first sc, (ch 1, skip next st, sc in next st) across changing to White in last sc: 88 sc.
Row 9: Ch 1, turn; sc in first sc, ★ working **behind** next ch-1, dc in st one row **below** ch-1, sc in next sc; repeat from ★ across changing to Black in last sc: 175 sts.
Row 10: Ch 1, turn; sc in first sc, ch 1, skip next dc, sc in next sc, ★ ch 1, skip next dc, working **behind** skipped dc, slip st in ch-1 sp one row **below** skipped dc, ch 2, sc in next sc, ch 1, skip next dc, sc in next sc; repeat from ★ across changing to White in last sc: 88 sc.
Row 11: Ch 1, turn; sc in first sc, working in **front** of next ch-1, dc in dc one row **below** ch-1, sc in next sc, ★ dc in skipped dc one row **below**, sc in next sc, working in **front** of next ch-1, dc in dc one row **below** ch-1, sc in next sc; repeat from ★ across, do **not** change color: 175 sts.
Row 12: Ch 1, turn; sc in first sc, (ch 1, skip next dc, sc in next sc) across changing to Black in last sc: 88 sc.
Row 13: Ch 1, turn; sc in first sc, working in **front** of next ch-1, dc in dc one row **below** ch-1, sc in next sc, ★ working **behind** next ch-1, dc in dc one row **below** ch-1, sc in next sc, working in **front** of next ch-1, dc in dc one row **below** ch-1, sc in next sc; repeat from ★ across changing to White in last sc: 175 sts.

Continued on page 116.

Row 14: Ch 1, turn; sc in first sc, ch 1, skip next dc, sc in next sc, ★ skip next dc, working **behind** skipped dc, dc in ch-1 sp one row **below** skipped dc, sc in next sc, ch 1, skip next dc, sc in next sc; repeat from ★ across; finish off: 44 ch-1 sps.

SECOND SIDE

Row 1: With **wrong** side facing and working in free loops of beginning ch (*Fig. 15b, page 140*), join Red with slip st in first ch; ch 1, sc in same st, (ch 1, skip next ch, sc in next ch) across changing to Black in last sc: 88 sc.
Rows 2-13: Work same as Rows 3-14 of First Side.
Note: Mark last row as bottom edge.

ASSEMBLY

With White and working through **both** loops, whipstitch Strips together (*Fig. 20b, page 142*).

EDGING

With **right** side facing, join White with slip st in any st; ch 3, dc evenly around, working 3 dc in each corner; join with slip st to top of beginning ch-3, finish off.

WINTER WARMER

For a luxurious throw that works up easily, crochet this rich comforter in any color to match your décor. Rows of cluster stitches create the simply beautiful design.

Finished Size: 49" x 68"

MATERIALS
Worsted Weight Yarn:
66 ounces, (1,870 grams, 3,730 yards)
Crochet hook, size G (4.00 mm) **or** size needed for gauge

GAUGE: In pattern, 15 sts = 4"; 8 rows = $3^1/_2$"

Gauge Swatch: $5^3/_4$"w x 4"h
Ch 23 **loosely**.
Work same as Afghan for 9 rows.
Finish off.

Note: Each row is worked across length of Afghan.

STITCH GUIDE

CLUSTER (uses next 5 dc)
★ YO, insert hook in **next** dc, YO and pull up a loop, YO and draw through 2 loops on hook; repeat from ★ 4 times **more**, YO and draw through all 6 loops on hook (*Figs. 12a & b, page 139*).

AFGHAN

Ch 258 **loosely**.
Row 1: Sc in back ridge of second ch from hook and each ch across (*Fig. 2b, page 137*): 257 sc.

Row 2 (Right side): Ch 3 **(counts as first dc, now and throughout)**, turn; skip next 2 sc, 5 dc in next sc, (skip next 4 sc, 5 dc in next sc) across to last 3 sc, skip next 2 sc, dc in last sc: 51 5-dc groups.
Note: Mark Row 2 as **right** side.
Row 3: Ch 5 **(counts as first dc plus ch 2, now and throughout)**, turn; work Cluster, (ch 4, work Cluster) across to last dc, ch 2, dc in last dc: 51 Clusters and 52 sps.
Row 4: Ch 1, turn; sc in first dc, 2 sc in next ch-2 sp, sc in next Cluster, (4 sc in next ch-4 sp, sc in next Cluster) across to last ch-2 sp, 2 sc in last ch-2 sp, sc in last dc: 257 sc.
Row 5: Ch 1, turn; sc in each sc across.
Row 6: Ch 3, turn; skip next 2 sc, 5 dc in next sc, (skip next 4 sc, 5 dc in next sc) across to last 3 sc, skip next 2 sc, dc in last sc: 51 5-dc groups.
Row 7: Ch 5, turn; work Cluster, (ch 4, work Cluster) across to last dc, ch 2, dc in last dc: 51 Clusters and 52 sps.
Row 8: Ch 1, turn; sc in first dc, 2 sc in next ch-2 sp, sc in next Cluster, (4 sc in next ch-4 sp, sc in next Cluster) across to last ch-2 sp, 2 sc in last ch-2 sp, sc in last dc: 257 sc.
Rows 9-112: Repeat Rows 5-8, 26 times.
Finish off.

Holding 8 strands of yarn together, add fringe in end of dc rows across short edges of Afghan (*Figs. 22b & d, page 142*).

STUNNING

This vivid throw will warm up your winter nights in front of the fire. Variegated yarn gives the wavy pattern a unique appearance, and flowing fringe incorporates the long yarn ends that are created when you change yarn colors.

Finished Size: 51¹/₂ " x 69"

MATERIALS
Worsted Weight Yarn:
Variegated - 28 ounces, (800 grams, 1,695 yards)
Black - 19 ounces, (540 grams, 1,245 yards)
Crochet hook, size I (5.50 mm) **or** size needed for gauge
Yarn needle

GAUGE: In pattern, one repeat = 3"
Each Strip = 5³/₄ " wide

Gauge Swatch: 9"w x 3"h
With Variegated, ch 32.
Work same as Strip First Side.

Note: Each row is worked across length of Strip. When joining yarn and finishing off, leave an 8" length to be worked into fringe.

STRIP (Make 9)
FIRST SIDE
With Variegated, ch 232.
Row 1 (Wrong side): Sc in second ch from hook, ch 1, skip next ch, sc in next ch, ch 1, skip next 2 chs, (dc, ch 3, dc) in next ch, ch 1, skip next 2 chs, sc in next ch, ch 1, ★ (skip next ch, sc in next ch, ch 1) twice, skip next 2 chs, (dc, ch 3, dc) in next ch, ch 1, skip next 2 chs, sc in next ch, ch 1; repeat from ★ across to last 2 chs, skip next ch, sc in last ch; finish off: 116 sts and 115 sps.
Note: Mark **back** of any stitch on Row 1 as **right** side.
Row 2: With **right** side facing, join Variegated with sc in first sc *(see Joining With Sc, page 140)*; sc in next ch-1 sp, ch 1, skip next sc, dc in next dc, ch 1, (dc, ch 1) 3 times in next ch-3 sp, dc in next dc, ch 1, ★ skip next ch-1 sp, (sc in next ch-1 sp, ch 1) twice, skip next sc, dc in next dc, ch 1, (dc, ch 1) 3 times in next ch-3 sp, dc in next dc, ch 1; repeat from ★ across to last 2 ch-1 sps, skip next ch-1 sp, sc in next ch-1 sp and in last sc; finish off: 163 sts and 160 ch-1 sps.

Row 3: With **wrong** side facing, join Variegated with sc in first sc; ch 1, skip next sc, (sc in next dc, ch 1) 5 times, ★ skip next ch-1 sp, sc in next ch-1 sp, ch 1, skip next sc, (sc in next dc, ch 1) 5 times; repeat from ★ across to last 2 sc, skip next sc, sc in last sc; finish off: 139 sc and 138 ch-1 sps.
Row 4: With **right** side facing, join Black with slip st in first sc; ch 4 **(counts as first tr, now and throughout)**, (dc in next sc, ch 1) twice, (dc, ch 1) 3 times in next sc, dc in next sc, ch 1, ★ dc in next 3 sc, ch 1, dc in next sc, ch 1, (dc, ch 1) 3 times in next sc, dc in next sc, ch 1; repeat from ★ across to last 2 sc, dc in next sc, tr in last sc; finish off: 185 sts and 138 ch-1 sps.
Row 5: With **wrong** side facing, join Variegated with sc in first tr; ch 1, skip next dc, (sc in next dc, ch 1) 5 times, ★ skip next dc, sc in next dc, ch 1, skip next dc, (sc in next dc, ch 1) 5 times; repeat from ★ across to last dc, skip last dc, sc in last tr; finish off: 139 sc and 138 ch-1 sps.
Row 6: With **right** side facing, join Black with slip st in first sc; ch 4, dc in next sc, ch 1, sc in next sc, ch 1, slip st in next sc, ch 1, sc in next sc, ch 1, ★ dc in next 3 sc, ch 1, sc in next sc, ch 1, slip st in next sc, ch 1, sc in next sc, ch 1; repeat from ★ across to last 2 sc, dc in next sc, tr in last sc; finish off: 139 sts and 92 ch-1 sps.

SECOND SIDE
Row 1: With **wrong** side facing and working in free loops of beginning ch *(Fig. 15b, page 140)*, join Variegated with sc in first ch; ch 1, skip next ch, sc in next ch, ch 1, skip next 2 chs, (dc, ch 3, dc) in next ch, ch 1, skip next 2 chs, sc in next ch, ch 1, ★ (skip next ch, sc in next ch, ch 1) twice, skip next 2 chs, (dc, ch 3, dc) in next ch, ch 1, skip next 2 chs, sc in next ch, ch 1; repeat from ★ 21 times **more**, skip next ch, sc in next ch; finish off: 116 sts and 115 sps.
Rows 2-6: Work same as First Side.

ASSEMBLY
With Black and working through **both** loops, whipstitch Strips together beginning in first tr and ending in last tr *(Fig. 20b, page 142)*.

Continued on page 120.

RIM

Row 1: With **wrong** side facing and working across long edge, join Black with sc in first tr; sc in next dc, (ch 1, skip next ch, sc in next st) 4 times, ★ ch 1, skip next dc, sc in next dc, (ch 1, skip next ch, sc in next st) 4 times; repeat from ★ across to last tr, sc in last tr; finish off: 117 sc and 114 ch-1 sps.

Row 2: With **right** side facing, join Black with slip st in first sc; ch 1, (slip st in next ch-1 sp, ch 1) across to last 2 sc, skip next sc, slip st in last sc; finish off. Repeat for Second Side.

Holding 3 strands of each color yarn together, add additional fringe evenly spaced across short edges of Afghan *(Figs. 22b & d, page 142)*.

CHRISTMAS COVER-UP

Wrap yourself in warmth with our plush seasonal comforter. Striped in the colors of Christmas, the throw is certain to temper winter's chill.

Finished Size: 49" x 66"

MATERIALS
Worsted Weight Yarn:
  Green - 20 ounces, (570 grams, 1,215 yards)
  Red - 19 ounces, (540 grams, 1,155 yards)
  Tan - 18 ounces, (510 grams, 1,095 yards)
Crochet hook, size I (5.50 mm) **or** size needed for gauge

GAUGE: In pattern, 13 sts = 4"; 12 rows = $4^1/4$"

Gauge Swatch: 4"w x $4^1/4$"h
Ch 14 **loosely**.
Work same as Afghan Body for 12 rows.
Finish off.

STITCH GUIDE

> **LONG DOUBLE CROCHET (abbreviated LDC)**
> YO, working **around** previous row *(Fig. 16, page 141)*, insert hook in sc one row **below** next dc, YO and pull up a loop even with loop on hook, (YO and draw through 2 loops on hook) twice *(Fig. 9, page 139)*.
>
> **EXTRA LONG DOUBLE CROCHET**
>   **(abbreviated Ex LDC)**
> YO, working **around** previous rows *(Fig. 16, page 141)*, insert hook in st 3 rows **below** next dc, YO and pull up a loop even with loop on hook, (YO and draw through 2 loops on hook) twice.

AFGHAN BODY
With Red, ch 158 **loosely**.
Row 1 (Right side): Sc in second ch from hook and in each ch across: 157 sc.
Note: Mark Row 1 as **right** side.
Row 2: Ch 3 **(counts as first dc, now and throughout)**, turn; dc in next sc and in each sc across.
Row 3: Ch 1, turn; sc in each dc across.
Row 4: Ch 3, turn; dc in next sc and in each sc across changing to Green in last dc *(Fig. 17a, page 141)*.
Row 5: Ch 1, turn; sc in first 3 dc, work Ex LDC, ★ sc in next 2 dc, work LDC, sc in next 2 dc, work Ex LDC; repeat from ★ across to last 3 dc, sc in last 3 dc.
Row 6: Ch 3, turn; dc in next sc and in each st across.
Row 7: Ch 1, turn; sc in each dc across.
Row 8: Ch 3, turn; dc in next sc and in each sc across changing to Tan in last dc.
Rows 9-11: Repeat Rows 5-7.
Row 12: Ch 3, turn; dc in next sc and in each sc across changing to Red in last dc.
Rows 13-15: Repeat Rows 5-7.
Rows 16-183: Repeat Rows 4-15, 14 times.
Row 184: Ch 3, turn; dc in next sc and in each sc across; finish off.

EDGING

Rnd 1: With **right** side facing, join Green with slip st in any corner; ch 1, sc evenly around Afghan working 3 sc in each corner; join with slip st to first sc.

Rnd 2: Ch 1, sc in each sc around working 3 sc in center sc of each corner 3-sc group; join with slip st to first sc, finish off.

BOLD PLAID

With its bold buffalo plaid, our cuddly comforter could be stitched in any color combination. The stately effect is quick to achieve holding two strands of yarn.

Finished Size: 53" x 68"

MATERIALS
Worsted Weight Yarn:
Black - 40 ounces, (1,140 grams, 2,810 yards)
Teal - 29 ounces, (820 grams, 2,040 yards)
Crochet hook, size N (9.00 mm) **or** size needed
for gauge

Note: Afghan is worked holding two strands of yarn together throughout.

GAUGE: In pattern, 12 dc = $5^3/_4$"
and 7 rows = $5^1/_4$"

Note: To work **color change**, work the last dc to within one step of completion, drop one strand of yarn, hook new yarn and remaining strand and draw through both loops on hook (*Fig. 17a, page 141*). Always keep unused color to **wrong** side. Do **not** cut yarn unless specified.
Start **each** new color change across Row 1 with a new skein of yarn. Work each additional row across to next dropped color, drop one strand of yarn and replace with yarn from dropped skein on previous row.
To prevent your skeins of yarn from twisting together when turning your work at the end of the row, turn all **right** side rows clockwise and all **wrong** side rows counterclockwise.

AFGHAN

With two strands of Black, ch 113 **loosely**.
Row 1 (Right side): 2 Dc in fifth ch from hook, (skip next ch, 2 dc in next ch) 5 times changing to one strand Black and one strand Teal in last dc, (skip next ch, 2 dc in next ch) 6 times changing to two strands Black in last dc, ★ (skip next ch, 2 dc in next ch) 6 times changing to one strand Black and one strand Teal in last dc, (skip next ch, 2 dc in next ch) 6 times changing to two strands Black in last dc; repeat from ★ 2 times **more**, skip next ch, (2 dc in next ch, skip next ch) 6 times, dc in last ch: 110 sts.
Note: Mark Row 1 as **right** side.

Continue to change colors in same manner throughout.
Rows 2-6: Ch 3 **(counts as first dc, now and throughout)**, turn; skip next dc, 2 dc in sp **before** next dc, (skip next 2 dc, 2 dc in sp **before** next dc) 5 times, ★ with one strand Black and one strand Teal, (skip next 2 dc, 2 dc in sp **before** next dc) 6 times, with two strands Black, (skip next 2 dc, 2 dc in sp **before** next dc) 6 times; repeat from ★ across to last 2 sts, skip next dc, dc in last st.
Row 7: Ch 3, turn; skip next dc, 2 dc in sp **before** next dc, (skip next 2 dc, 2 dc in sp **before** next dc) 5 times, ★ with one strand Black and one strand Teal, (skip next 2 dc, 2 dc in sp **before** next dc) 6 times, with two strands Black, (skip next 2 dc, 2 dc in sp **before** next dc) 6 times; repeat from ★ across to last 2 dc, skip next dc, dc in last dc changing to one strand Black and one strand Teal, cut Black just dropped.
Rows 8-13: Ch 3, turn; skip next dc, 2 dc in sp **before** next dc, (skip next 2 dc, 2 dc in sp **before** next dc) 5 times, ★ with two strands Teal, (skip next 2 dc, 2 dc in sp **before** next dc) 6 times, with one strand Teal and one strand Black, (skip next 2 dc, 2 dc in sp **before** next dc) 6 times; repeat from ★ across to last 2 dc, skip next dc, dc in last dc.
Row 14: Ch 3, turn; skip next dc, 2 dc in sp **before** next dc, (skip next 2 dc, 2 dc in sp **before** next dc) 5 times, ★ with two strands Teal, (skip next 2 dc, 2 dc in sp **before** next dc) 6 times, with one strand Teal and one strand Black, (skip next 2 dc, 2 dc in sp **before** next dc) 6 times; repeat from ★ across to last 2 dc, skip next dc, dc in last dc changing to two strands Black, cut Teal just dropped.
Rows 15-20: Ch 3, turn; skip next dc, 2 dc in sp **before** next dc, (skip next 2 dc, 2 dc in sp **before** next dc) 5 times, ★ with one strand Black and one strand Teal, (skip next 2 dc, 2 dc in sp **before** next dc) 6 times, with two strands Black, (skip next 2 dc, 2 dc in sp **before** next dc) 6 times; repeat from ★ across to last 2 dc, skip next dc, dc in last dc.

Row 21: Ch 3, turn; skip next dc, 2 dc in sp **before** next dc, (skip next 2 dc, 2 dc in sp **before** next dc) 5 times, ★ with one strand Black and one strand Teal, (skip next 2 dc, 2 dc in sp **before** next dc) 6 times, with two strands Black, (skip next 2 dc, 2 dc in sp **before** next dc) 6 times; repeat from ★ across to last 2 dc, skip next dc, dc in last dc changing to one strand Black and one strand Teal, cut Black just dropped.
Rows 22-90: Repeat Rows 8-21, 4 times; then repeat Rows 8-20 once **more**.

Row 91: Ch 3, turn; skip next dc, 2 dc in sp **before** next dc, (skip next 2 dc, 2 dc in sp **before** next dc) 5 times, ★ with one strand Black and one strand Teal, (skip next 2 dc, 2 dc in sp **before** next dc) 6 times, with two strands Black, (skip next 2 dc, 2 dc in sp **before** next dc) 6 times; repeat from ★ across to last 2 dc, skip next dc, dc in last dc; finish off.

With Black and using three 16" strands of yarn held together, add fringe in each st across short edges of Afghan (*Figs. 22a & c, page 142*).

123

DASHING THROW

Deep blue and pure white come together to create this striking winter afghan.
Simple in its design, the easy throw works up in strips for a truly relaxing project.

Finished Size: 45" x 68"

MATERIALS
Worsted Weight Yarn:
White - 34 ounces, (970 grams, 2,330 yards)
Blue - 29 ounces, (820 grams, 1,990 yards)
Crochet hook, size G (4.00 mm) **or** size needed
for gauge
Yarn needle

GAUGE: 16 dc and 8 rows = 4"
Each Strip = 2³/₄" wide

STITCH GUIDE

DECREASE
Pull up a loop in next st on same Strip **and** in
next st on next Strip, YO and draw through all
3 loops on hook **(counts as one sc)**.
FRONT POST HALF DOUBLE CROCHET
(abbreviated FPhdc)
YO, insert hook from **front** to **back** around post
of st indicated *(Fig. 10, page 139)*, YO and pull
up a loop, YO and draw through all 3 loops on
hook. Skip st behind FPhdc.
FRONT POST TREBLE CROCHET
(abbreviated FPtr)
YO twice, insert hook from **front** to **back** around
post of st indicated *(Fig. 10, page 139)*, YO and
pull up a loop, (YO and draw through 2 loops
on hook) 3 times. Skip st behind FPtr.

STRIP (Make 16)
With White, ch 257 **loosely**.
Rnd 1 (Right side): 2 Sc in second ch from hook, sc
in next 127 chs, 2 sc in next ch, sc in each ch across
to last ch, 3 sc in last ch; working in free loops of
beginning ch *(Fig. 15b, page 140)*, sc in next 127 chs,
2 sc in next ch, sc in next 126 chs and in same ch as
first sc changing to Blue in last sc *(Fig. 17a,
page 141)*; join with slip st to first sc: 516 sc.
Note: Mark last sc made on Rnd 1 as **right** side and
bottom edge.

Rnd 2: Ch 1, 2 sc in same st and in next sc, † ch 1,
(skip next sc, sc in next sc, ch 1) 127 times †, skip
next sc, 2 sc in each of next 3 sc, repeat from † to †
once, skip next sc, 2 sc in last sc; join with slip st to
first sc: 266 sc and 256 ch-1 sps.
Rnd 3: Ch 3 **(counts as first dc)**, dc in same st, 2 dc
in each of next 2 sc, † dc in next sc and in next
ch-1 sp, working around bars of beginning ch
(Fig. 1), skip first bar, work FPtr around next bar,
★ dc in next ch-1 sp, skip next bar, work FPtr around
next bar; repeat from ★ across to last bar, leave last
bar unworked, dc in next ch-1 sp and in next sc †,
2 dc in each of next 4 sc, repeat from † to † once,
2 dc in last sc changing to White in last dc; join with
slip st to first dc: 254 FPtr and 276 dc.

Fig. 1

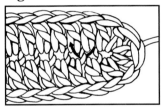

Rnd 4: Ch 1, 2 sc in same st and in next dc, † 3 sc in
next dc, 2 sc in each of next 2 dc, sc in next 3 dc,
work FPhdc around next FPtr, (sc in next dc, work
FPhdc around next FPtr) 126 times, sc in next 3 dc †,
2 sc in each of next 3 dc, repeat from † to † once,
2 sc in last dc; join with slip st to Back Loop Only of
first sc *(Fig. 14, page 140)*: 544 sts.
Rnd 5: Ch 1, working in Back Loops Only, sc in
same st and in next 12 sc, place marker around last
sc made for joining placement, sc in next 256 sts,
place marker around last sc made for joining
placement, sc in next 16 sc, place marker around last
sc made for joining placement, sc in next 256 sts,
place marker around last sc made for joining
placement, sc in last 3 sc; join with slip st to **both**
loops of first sc, finish off.

ASSEMBLY
With White, placing bottom edges at same end and
working through **inside** loops only, whipstitch
Strips together *(Fig. 20a, page 142)*, beginning at first
marker and ending at next marker. Do **not** remove
markers on outside edge of first Strip.

EDGING

With **right** side of short end facing and working in both loops, join Blue with sc in first sc after marked sc at top of first Strip *(see Joining With Sc, page 140)*, remove all markers; ch 3, ★ skip next sc, (sc in next sc, ch 3, skip next sc) 6 times, decrease, ch 3; repeat from ★ 14 times **more**, (skip next sc, sc in next sc, ch 3) across to within 2 sc of next joining, skip next sc, decrease, ch 3, † skip next sc, (sc in next sc, ch 3, skip next sc) 6 times, decrease, ch 3 †, repeat from † to † 13 times **more**, skip next sc, (sc in next sc, ch 3, skip next sc) across; join with slip st to first sc, finish off.

EVERGREEN

This gorgeous wrap will provide a bit of evergreen appeal during the stark winter season. Yarn ends — left over from joining and finishing off — are worked into the fringe of our hearty, worsted weight throw.

Finished Size: 46" x 61"

MATERIALS

Worsted Weight Yarn:
Dk Green - 16$^1/_2$ ounces,
(470 grams, 1,075 yards)
Green - 15$^1/_2$ ounces, (440 grams, 1,010 yards)
Lt Green - 15$^1/_2$ ounces,
(440 grams, 1,010 yards)
Crochet hook, size J (6.00 mm) **or** size needed for gauge

GAUGE: In pattern,
[(LDC, ch 1, LDC), (dc, ch 1, dc)] 3 times
and 12 rows = 4$^1/_2$ "

Gauge Swatch: 5"w x 4$^1/_2$ "h
With Dk Green, ch 14 **loosely**.
Work same as Afghan for 12 rows.
Finish off.

Note: Each row is worked across length of Afghan. When joining yarn and finishing off, leave an 8" end to be worked into fringe.

COLOR SEQUENCE

3 Rows Dk Green, ★ 2 rows **each**: Green, Lt Green, Dk Green; repeat from ★ 19 times **more**.

STITCH GUIDE

> **LONG DOUBLE CROCHET** *(abbreviated LDC)*
> YO, working **around** previous row *(Fig. 16, page 141)*, insert hook in ch-1 sp indicated, YO and pull up a loop even with loop on hook *(Fig. 9, page 139)*, (YO and draw through 2 loops on hook) twice.

AFGHAN

With Dk Green, ch 162 **loosely**.
Row 1 (Right side): Sc in second ch from hook and in each ch across: 161 sc.
Note: Mark Row 1 as **right** side.
Row 2: Ch 4 **(counts as first dc plus ch 1, now and throughout)**, turn; dc in same st, ★ skip next sc, (dc, ch 1, dc) in next sc; repeat from ★ across: 81 ch-1 sps.

Row 3: Ch 1, turn; sc in first dc, [skip next dc, sc in sp **before** next dc *(Fig. 18, page 141)* and in next ch-1 sp] across to last 3 dc, skip next dc, sc in sp **before** next dc, skip next dc, sc in last dc; finish off: 161 sc.
Row 4: With **right** side facing, join next color with slip st in first sc; ch 4, work LDC in first ch-1 sp 2 rows **below**, skip next sc, (dc, ch 1, dc) in next sc, ★ skip next sc, work (LDC, ch 1, LDC) in ch-1 sp one row **below** next sc, skip next sc, (dc, ch 1, dc) in next sc; repeat from ★ across to last 2 sc, skip next sc, work LDC in last ch-1 sp 2 rows **below**, ch 1, dc in last sc: 80 LDC and 82 dc.
Row 5: Ch 1, turn; sc in first dc, (skip next dc, sc in sp **before** next dc and in next ch-1 sp) across to last 3 dc, skip next dc, sc in sp **before** next dc, skip next dc, sc in last dc; finish off: 161 sc.
Row 6: With **wrong** side facing, join next color with slip st in first sc; ch 4, work LDC in first ch-1 sp 2 rows **below**, skip next sc, (dc, ch 1, dc) in next sc, ★ skip next sc, work (LDC, ch 1, LDC) in ch-1 sp one row **below** next sc, skip next sc, (dc, ch 1, dc) in next sc; repeat from ★ across to last 2 sc, skip next sc, work LDC in last ch-1 sp 2 rows **below**, ch 1, dc in last sc: 80 LDC and 82 dc.
Row 7: Ch 1, turn; sc in first dc, (skip next dc, sc in sp **before** next dc and in next ch-1 sp) across to last 3 dc, skip next dc, sc in sp **before** next dc, skip next dc, sc in last dc; finish off: 161 sc.
Row 8: With **right** side facing, join next color with slip st in first sc; ch 4, work LDC in first ch-1 sp 2 rows **below**, skip next sc, (dc, ch 1, dc) in next sc, ★ skip next sc, work (LDC, ch 1, LDC) in ch-1 sp one row **below** next sc, skip next sc, (dc, ch 1, dc) in next sc; repeat from ★ across to last 2 sc, skip next sc, work LDC in last ch-1 sp 2 rows **below**, ch 1, dc in last sc: 80 LDC and 82 dc.
Rows 9-122: Repeat Rows 5-8, 28 times; then repeat Rows 5 and 6 once **more**.
Row 123: Ch 1, turn; sc in first dc and in each st across; finish off.

Using 6 strands of corresponding color held together, add fringe in end of each dc row across short edges of Afghan *(Figs. 22b & d, page 142)*.

CHAIN OF HEARTS

Accented with romantic hearts, this lovely afghan will be wonderful when you're wrapped up in dreams of someone you love! The heartwarming cover-up is sure to become a sentimental favorite.

Finished Size: 47" x 60"

MATERIALS
Worsted Weight Yarn:
49 ounces, (1,390 grams, 3,080 yards)
Crochet hook, size I (5.50 mm) **or** size needed for gauge

GAUGE: In pattern, 14 sts and 13 rows = 4"

Gauge Swatch: 9" x 4"
Ch 32 **loosely**.
Rows 1-13: Work same as Afghan: 31 sts.

Note: Afghan is worked from side to side. Always join yarn and finish off leaving a 7" end for fringe.

AFGHAN
Ch 212 **loosely**.
Row 1 (Right side): Sc in Back Loop Only of second ch from hook and in each ch across *(Fig. 14, page 140)*; finish off: 211 sc.
Note: Mark Row 1 as **right** side.
Work sc in Back Loops Only throughout.
Rows 2-4: With **right** side facing, join yarn with slip st in first sc; ch 1, sc in each sc across; finish off.
Row 5: With **right** side facing, join yarn with slip st in first sc; ch 1, sc in first 9 sc, working in free loops, dc in sc **below** next sc *(Fig. 1)*, skip sc behind dc **(now and throughout)**, (sc in next 11 sc, dc in sc **below** next sc) across to last 9 sc, sc in last 9 sc; finish off: 17 dc.

Fig. 1

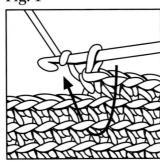

Row 6: With **right** side facing, join yarn with slip st in first sc; ch 1, sc in first 8 sc, dc in sc **below** next sc, sc in next dc, dc in sc **below** next sc, ★ sc in next 9 sc, dc in sc **below** next sc, sc in next dc, dc in sc **below** next sc; repeat from ★ across to last 8 sc, sc in last 8 sc; finish off: 34 dc.
Row 7: With **right** side facing, join yarn with slip st in first sc; ch 1, sc in first 7 sc, dc in sc **below** next sc, sc in next 3 sts, dc in sc **below** next sc, ★ sc in next 7 sc, dc in sc **below** next sc, sc in next 3 sts, dc in sc **below** next sc; repeat from ★ across to last 7 sc, sc in last 7 sc, finish off.
Row 8: With **right** side facing, join yarn with slip st in first sc; ch 1, sc in first 6 sc, dc in sc **below** next sc, (sc in next 5 sts, dc in sc **below** next sc) across to last 6 sc, sc in last 6 sc; finish off.
Row 9: With **right** side facing, join yarn with slip st in first sc; ch 1, sc in first 5 sc, dc in sc **below** next sc, sc in next 7 sts, dc in sc **below** next sc, ★ sc in next 3 sc, dc in sc **below** next sc, sc in next 7 sts, dc in sc **below** next sc; repeat from ★ across to last 5 sc, sc in last 5 sc; finish off.
Row 10: With **right** side facing, join yarn with slip st in first sc; ch 1, sc in first 4 sc, dc in sc **below** next sc, sc in next 9 sts, dc in sc **below** next sc, ★ sc in next sc, dc in sc **below** next sc, sc in next 9 sts, dc in sc **below** next sc; repeat from ★ across to last 4 sc, sc in last 4 sc; finish off.
Row 11: With **right** side facing, join yarn with slip st in first sc; ch 1, sc in first 3 sc, dc in sc **below** next sc, (sc in next 11 sts, dc in sc **below** next sc) across to last 3 sc, sc in last 3 sc; finish off: 18 dc.
Row 12: With **right** side facing, join yarn with slip st in first sc; ch 1, sc in first 3 sc, dc around post of next dc *(Fig. 10, page 139)*, ★ sc in next 5 sc, dc in sc **below** next sc, sc in next 5 sc, dc around post of next dc; repeat from ★ across to last 3 sc, sc in last 3 sc; finish off: 35 dc.

Continued on page 130.

Row 13: With **right** side facing, join yarn with slip st in first sc; ch 1, sc in first 3 sc, ★ sc in next dc, dc in sc **below** next sc, sc in next 3 sc, dc in sc **below** next sc; repeat from ★ across to last 4 sts, sc in last 4 sts; finish off: 68 dc.

Row 14: With **right** side facing, join yarn with slip st in first sc; ch 1, sc in first 5 sts, dc in each sc **below** next 3 sc, (sc in next 3 sts, dc in each sc **below** next 3 sc) across to last 5 sts, sc in last 5 sts; finish off: 102 dc.

Rows 15-17: With **right** side facing, join yarn with slip st in first sc; ch 1, sc in each st across; finish off: 211 sc.

Repeat Rows 5-17 until Afghan measures approximately 46³/₄", ending by working Row 17, then repeat Row 17 once **more**.

Add fringe in end of rows across short edges of Afghan *(Figs. 22b & d, page 142)*.

DOUBLE COZY

Take the chill out of those cold winter nights with this cozy afghan! It works up quickly because you hold two strands of yarn together as you crochet.

Finished Size: 48" x 68"

MATERIALS
   Worsted Weight Yarn:
      88 ounces, (2,550 grams, 5,540 yards)
   Crochet hook, size Q (15.00 mm) **or** size needed for gauge

GAUGE: (Sc, ch 2, sc) twice and 4 rows = 3"

Note: Afghan is worked holding two strands of yarn together throughout.

AFGHAN

Ch 68 **loosely**.

Row 1 (Right side): (Sc, ch 2, sc) in fourth ch from hook, [skip next ch, (sc, ch 2, sc) in next ch] across to last 2 chs, skip next ch, sc in last ch: 32 ch-2 sps.
Note: Mark Row 1 as **right** side.

Row 2: Ch 3, turn; (sc, ch 2, sc) in next ch-2 sp and in each ch-2 sp across, sc in last sp (working over beginning ch).

Row 3: Ch 3, turn; (sc, ch 2, sc) in next ch-2 sp and in each ch-2 sp across, sc in last sp (working over turning ch).

Repeat Row 3 until Afghan measures approximately 67¹/₂" from beginning ch, ending by working a **wrong** side row; do **not** finish off.

Last Row: Ch 2, turn; (sc in next ch-2 sp, ch 1) across, sc in last sp; finish off.

Add fringe across short edges of Afghan *(Figs. 22a & c, page 142)*.

TWILIGHT SNOWFLAKES

*Snowflake motifs on a background of the deepest blue are reminders of
a wondrous evening snowfall. Crochet all the motifs individually,
then use the placement diagram to assemble this dreamy wrap.*

Finished Size: 49" x 63"

MATERIALS
   Worsted Weight Yarn:
      Dk Blue - 25³/₄ ounces, (730 grams, 1,765 yards)
      White - 13¹/₄ ounces, (380 grams, 910 yards)
      Blue - 12¹/₂ ounces, (360 grams, 855 yards)
      Lt Blue - 11¹/₂ ounces, (330 grams, 790 yards)
   Crochet hook, size H (5.00 mm) **or** size needed
      for gauge
   Yarn needle

GAUGE: Each Motif = 7"
            (straight edge to straight edge)
            Fill-In Motif = 3¹/₄ " square

Gauge Swatch: 4" diameter
Work same as Motif through Rnd 3.

STITCH GUIDE

FRONT POST DOUBLE CROCHET
   (abbreviated FPdc)
YO, insert hook from **front** to **back** around post
of st indicated *(Fig. 10, page 139)*, YO and pull
up a loop, (YO and draw through 2 loops on
hook) twice. Skip dc behind FPdc.
CLUSTER (uses next 3 sts)
Insert hook in next sc, YO and pull up a loop,
YO, insert hook from **front** to **back** around post
of next tr *(Fig. 10, page 139)*, YO and pull up a
loop, YO and draw through 2 loops on hook,
insert hook in next sc, YO and pull up a loop,
YO and draw through all 4 loops on hook
(Figs. 12a & b, page 139).

DOUBLE CROCHET CLUSTER
   (abbreviated dc Cluster) (uses next 3 dc)
YO, insert hook in next dc, YO and pull up a
loop, YO and draw through 2 loops on hook,
YO, insert hook from **front** to **back** around post
of next dc *(Fig. 10, page 139)*, YO and pull up a
loop, YO and draw through 2 loops on hook,
YO, insert hook in next dc, YO and pull up a
loop, YO and draw through 2 loops on hook, YO
and draw through all 4 loops on hook
(Figs. 12a & b, page 139).
**FRONT POST DOUBLE CROCHET
CLUSTER** *(abbreviated FPdc Cluster)*
   (uses next 2 Clusters and ch-1 sp)
† YO, insert hook from **front** to **back** around
post of **next** Cluster *(Fig. 10, page 139)*, YO and
pull up a loop, YO and draw through 2 loops on
hook †, YO, insert hook in next ch-1 sp, YO and
pull up a loop, YO and draw through 2 loops on
hook, repeat from † to † once, YO and draw
through all 4 loops on hook *(Figs. 12a & b,
page 139)*.
FRONT POST TREBLE CLUSTER
   (abbreviated FPtr Cluster)
      (uses same st and next 3 sts)
YO twice, insert hook from **front** to **back** around
post of same FPdc as fourth leg of last
FPtr Cluster *(Fig. 10, page 139)*, YO and pull up
a loop, (YO and draw through 2 loops on hook)
twice, ★ YO, insert hook in **next** dc, YO and pull
up a loop, YO and draw through 2 loops on
hook; repeat from ★ once **more**, YO twice, insert
hook from **front** to **back** around post of next
FPdc, YO and pull up a loop, (YO and draw
through 2 loops on hook) twice, YO and draw
through all 5 loops on hook *(Figs. 12a & b,
page 139)*.

Continued on page 134.

MOTIF (Make 63)

With White, ch 4; join with slip st to form a ring.

Rnd 1 (Right side): Ch 3 **(counts as first dc, now and throughout)**, 15 dc in ring; join with slip st to first dc, finish off: 16 dc.

Note: Mark Rnd 1 as **right** side.

Rnd 2: With **right** side facing, join Lt Blue with slip st from **front** to **back** around post of any dc *(Fig. 10, page 139)*; ch 3 **(counts as first FPdc)**, 2 dc in next dc, (work FPdc around next dc, 2 dc in next dc) around; join with slip st to first FPdc: 24 sts.

Rnd 3: Slip st from **front** to **back** around post of same st, ch 4, † ★ YO, insert hook in **next** dc, YO and pull up a loop, YO and draw through 2 loops on hook; repeat from ★ once **more**, YO twice †, insert hook from **front** to **back** around post of next FPdc, YO and pull up a loop, (YO and draw through 2 loops on hook) twice, YO and draw through all 4 loops on hook **(Beginning FPtr Cluster made)**, ch 7, (work FPtr Cluster, ch 7) 6 times, YO twice, insert hook from **front** to **back** around post of same FPdc as fourth leg of last FPtr Cluster, YO and pull up a loop, (YO and draw through 2 loops on hook) twice, repeat from † to † once, working **above** first leg of Beginning FPtr Cluster, insert hook from **front** to **back** around post of same FPdc as Beginning FPtr Cluster, YO and pull up a loop, (YO and draw through 2 loops on hook) twice, YO and draw through all 5 loops on hook, ch 7; join with slip st to top of Beginning FPtr Cluster, finish off: 8 ch-7 sps.

Rnd 4: With **right** side facing, join White with sc in any ch-7 sp *(see Joining With Sc, page 140)*; working in **front** of ch-7 *(Fig. 16, page 141)*, tr in next FPdc on Rnd 2, 3 sc in same sp on Rnd 3, working in **front** of same ch-7, tr in same st on Rnd 2 as last tr, ★ sc in same sp and in next ch-7 sp on Rnd 3, working in **front** of ch-7, tr in next FPdc on Rnd 2, 3 sc in same sp on Rnd 3, working in **front** of same ch-7, tr in same st on Rnd 2 as last tr; repeat from ★ around, sc in same sp on Rnd 3; join with slip st to first sc, finish off: 56 sts.

Rnd 5: With **right** side facing, join Blue with slip st in center sc of any 3-sc group; ch 6, dc in same st, ch 1, (work Cluster, ch 1) twice, ★ (dc, ch 3, dc) in next sc, ch 1, (work Cluster, ch 1) twice; repeat from ★ around; join with slip st to third ch of beginning ch-6, finish off: 16 Clusters, 16 dc, and 32 sps.

Rnd 6: With **right** side facing, join Dk Blue with slip st in any ch-3 sp; ch 6, dc in same sp, ch 1, work FPdc around next dc, ch 1, work FPdc Cluster, ch 1, work FPdc around next dc, ch 1, ★ (dc, ch 3, dc) in next ch-3 sp, ch 1, work FPdc around next dc, ch 1, work FPdc Cluster, ch 1, work FPdc around next dc, ch 1; repeat from ★ around; join with slip st to third ch of beginning ch-6: 40 sts and 40 sps.

Rnd 7: Slip st in first ch-3 sp, ch 1, 3 sc in same sp, sc in next ch-1 sp, (sc in next st and in next ch-1 sp) 3 times, ★ 3 sc in next ch-3 sp, sc in next ch-1 sp, (sc in next st and in next ch-1 sp) 3 times; repeat from ★ around; join with slip st to first sc, finish off: 80 sc.

FILL-IN MOTIF (Make 48)

With White, ch 4; join with slip st to form a ring.

Rnd 1: Ch 3, 15 dc in ring; join with slip st to first dc, finish off: 16 dc.

Note: Mark Rnd 1 as **right** side.

Rnd 2: With **right** side facing, join Blue with slip st from **front** to **back** around post of any dc; ch 6, work FPdc around same st, ch 2, work dc Cluster, ch 2, ★ work (FPdc, ch 3, FPdc) around next dc, ch 2, work dc Cluster, ch 2; repeat from ★ 2 times **more**; join with slip st to third ch of beginning ch-6, finish off: 12 sts and 12 sps.

Rnd 3: With **right** side facing, join Dk Blue with sc in any ch-3 sp; 2 sc in same sp, sc in next FPdc, 2 sc in next ch-2 sp, sc in next dc Cluster, 2 sc in next ch-2 sp, sc in next FPdc, ★ 3 sc in next ch-3 sp, sc in next FPdc, 2 sc in next ch-2 sp, sc in next dc Cluster, 2 sc in next ch-2 sp, sc in next FPdc; repeat from ★ 2 times **more**; join with slip st to first sc, finish off leaving a 24" length for sewing: 40 sc.

ASSEMBLY

With Dk Blue, using Placement Diagram as a guide, and working through **both** loops, whipstitch Motifs together forming 7 vertical strips of 9 Motifs each *(Fig. 20b, page 142)*, beginning in center ch of first corner ch-3 and ending in center ch of next corner ch-3; then whipstitch strips together in same manner.

Whipstitch Fill-In Motifs in each sp between joined Motifs.

Using photo as a guide for placement and holding 9 strands of Dk Blue yarn together, add fringe in each ch-3 sp across short edges of Afghan *(Figs. 22a & c, page 142)*.

PLACEMENT DIAGRAM

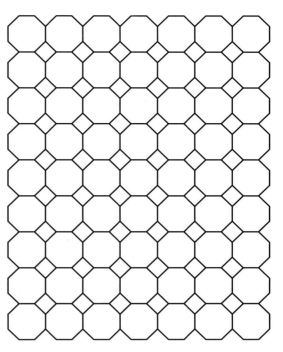

GENERAL INSTRUCTIONS

ABBREVIATIONS

BP	Back Post	hdc	half double crochet(s)
BPtr	Back Post treble crochet(s)	htr	half treble crochet(s)
ch(s)	chain(s)	LDC	Long double crochet(s)
dc	double crochet(s)	Lt	Light
Dk	Dark	mm	millimeters
dtr	double treble crochet(s)	Rnd(s)	Round(s)
Ex LDC	extra long double crochet(s)	sc	single crochet(s)
FP	Front Post	sp(s)	space(s)
FPdc	Front Post double crochet(s)	st(s)	stitch(es)
FPhdc	Front Post half double crochet(s)	tr	treble crochet(s)
FPtr	Front Post treble crochet(s)	YO	yarn over

★ — work instructions following ★ as many **more** times as indicated in addition to the first time.

† to † or ♥ to ♥ — work all instructions from first † to second † or from first ♥ to second ♥ **as many** times as specified.

( ) or [ ] — work enclosed instructions **as many** times as specified by the number immediately following **or** work all enclosed instructions in the stitch or space indicated **or** contains explanatory remarks.

colon (:) — the number(s) given after a colon at the end of a row or round denote(s) the number of stitches you should have on that row or round.

TERMS

chain loosely — work the chain **only** loose enough for the hook to pass through the chain easily when working the next row or round into the chain.

leg — the first or second part of a pattern stitch.

post — the vertical shaft of a stitch.

right side vs. wrong side — the right side of your work is the side that will show when the piece is finished.

work across or around — continue working in the established pattern.

GAUGE

Gauge is the number of stitches and rows or rounds per inch and is used to determine the finished size of an Afghan. All patterns in this book specify the gauge that you must match to ensure proper size and to ensure that you will have enough yarn to complete your Afghan.

Hook size given in instructions is merely a guide. Because everyone crochets differently — loosely, tightly, or somewhere in between — the finished size can vary, even when crocheters use the very same pattern, yarn, and hook.

Before beginning your Afghan, it is absolutely necessary for you to crochet a gauge swatch in the pattern stitch indicated and with the weight of yarn and hook size suggested. Your swatch must be large enough to measure your gauge. Lay your swatch on a hard, smooth, flat surface. Then measure it, counting your stitches and rows or rounds carefully. If your swatch is smaller than specified or you have too many stitches per inch, try again with a larger size hook; if your swatch is larger than specified or you don't have enough stitches per inch, try again with a smaller size hook. Keep trying until you find the size that will give you the specified gauge. **DO NOT HESITATE TO CHANGE HOOK SIZE TO OBTAIN CORRECT GAUGE**. Once proper gauge is obtained, measure the width of the Afghan approximately every 3" to be sure gauge remains consistent.

BASIC STITCH GUIDE

CHAIN (abbreviated ch)

To work a chain stitch, begin with a slip knot on the hook. Bring the yarn **over** hook from **back** to **front**, catching the yarn with the hook and turning the hook slightly toward you to keep the yarn from slipping off. Draw the yarn through the slip knot (*Fig. 1*).

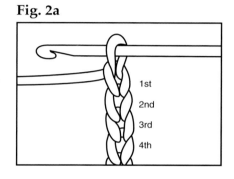

Fig. 1

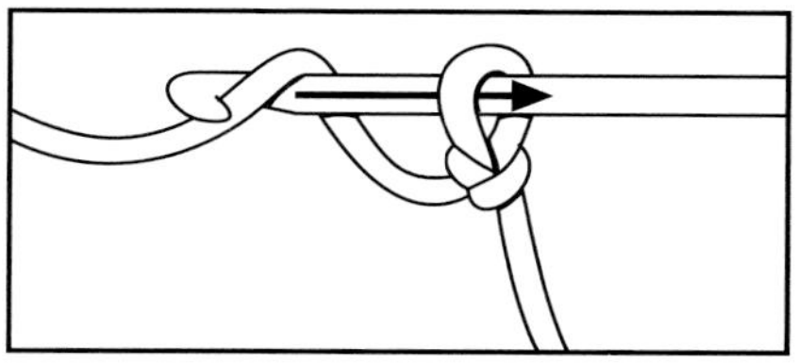

WORKING INTO THE CHAIN

When beginning a first row of crochet in a chain, always skip the first chain from the hook and work into the second chain from hook (for single crochet), third chain from hook (for half double crochet), or fourth chain from hook (for double crochet), etc. (*Fig. 2a*).

Fig. 2a

Method 1: Insert hook into back ridge of each chain indicated (*Fig. 2b*).
Method 2: Insert hook under top loop **and** the back ridge of each chain indicated (*Fig. 2c*).

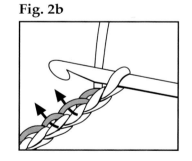

Fig. 2b

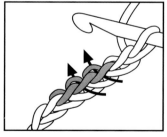

Fig. 2c

SLIP STITCH (abbreviated slip st)

This stitch is used to attach new yarn, to join work, or to move the yarn across a group of stitches without adding height.
Insert hook in stitch or space indicated, YO and draw through stitch **and** loop on hook (*Fig. 3*).

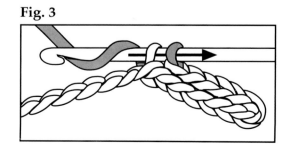

Fig. 3

SINGLE CROCHET (abbreviated sc)

Insert hook in stitch or space indicated, YO and pull up a loop, YO and draw through both loops on hook (*Fig. 4*).

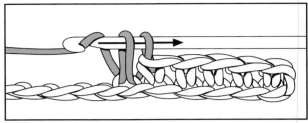

Fig. 4

HALF DOUBLE CROCHET

(abbreviated hdc)

YO, insert hook in stitch or space indicated, YO and pull up a loop, YO and draw through all 3 loops on hook (*Fig. 5*).

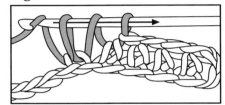

Fig. 5

DOUBLE CROCHET (abbreviated dc)

YO, insert hook in stitch or space indicated, YO and pull up a loop (3 loops on hook), YO and draw through 2 loops on hook (*Fig. 6a*), YO and draw through remaining 2 loops on hook (*Fig. 6b*).

Fig. 6a

Fig. 6b

TREBLE CROCHET (abbreviated tr)

YO twice, insert hook in stitch or space indicated, YO and pull up a loop (4 loops on hook) (*Fig. 7a*), (YO and draw through 2 loops on hook) 3 times (*Fig. 7b*).

Fig. 7a

Fig. 7b

DOUBLE TREBLE CROCHET

(abbreviated dtr)

YO 3 times, insert hook in stitch or space indicated, YO and pull up a loop (5 loops on hook) (*Fig. 8a*), (YO and draw through 2 loops on hook) 4 times (*Fig. 8b*).

Fig. 8a

Fig. 8b

PATTERN STITCHES

LONG DOUBLE CROCHET
(abbreviated LDC)
Work double crochet, inserting hook in stitch or space indicated in instructions *(Fig. 9)*, and pulling up a loop even with loop on hook; complete stitch.

Fig. 9

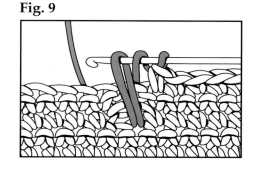

POST STITCH
Work around post of stitch indicated, inserting hook in direction of arrow *(Fig. 10)*.

Fig. 10

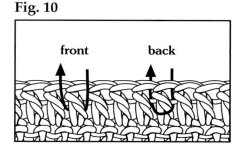

front   back

CLUSTER
A Cluster can be worked all in the same stitch or space *(Figs. 11a & b)*, **or** across several stitches *(Figs. 12a & b)*.

Fig. 11a

Fig. 11b

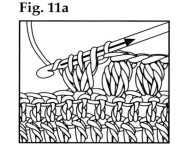

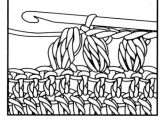

Fig. 12a

Fig. 12b

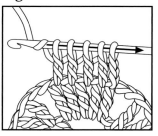

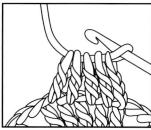

PUFF STITCH
★ YO, insert hook in stitch or space indicated, YO and pull up a loop even with loop on hook; repeat from ★ as many times as specified, YO and draw through all loops on hook *(Fig. 13)*.

Fig. 13

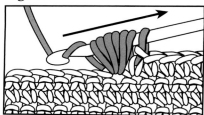

STITCHING TIPS

MARKERS
Markers are used to help distinguish the right side of the Afghan **or** to identify a specific stitch to be worked into later. Place a 2" scrap piece of yarn around a stitch on the row or round indicated, removing the marker after the Afghan is completed **or** as indicated in the instructions.

JOINING WITH SC
When instructed to join with sc, begin with a slip knot on hook. Insert hook in stitch or space indicated, YO and pull up a loop, YO and draw through both loops on hook.

JOINING WITH DC
When instructed to join with dc, begin with a slip knot on hook. YO, holding loop on hook, insert hook in stitch or space indicated, YO and pull up a loop (3 loops on hook), (YO and draw through 2 loops on hook) twice.

BACK OR FRONT LOOP ONLY
Work only in loop(s) indicated by arrow *(Fig. 14)*.

Fig. 14

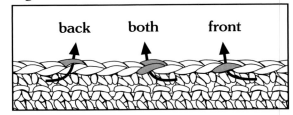

FREE LOOPS
After working in Back or Front Loops Only on a row or round, there will be a ridge of unused loops. These are called the free loops. Later, when instructed to work in the free loops of the same row or round, work in these loops *(Fig. 15a)*.
When instructed to work in a free loop of a beginning chain, work in loop indicated by arrow *(Fig. 15b)*.

Fig. 15a

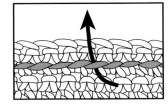

Fig. 15b

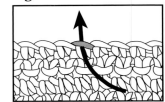

WORKING IN FRONT OF, AROUND, OR BEHIND A STITCH

Work in stitch or space indicated, inserting hook in direction of arrow *(Fig. 16)*.

Fig. 16

CHANGING COLORS

Work the last stitch to within one step of completion, hook new yarn *(Fig. 17a)* and draw through loops on hook. Cut old yarn and work over both ends unless otherwise specified. When working in rounds or changing colors with a slip st, drop old yarn; using new yarn, join with slip stitch to first stitch *(Fig. 17b)*.

Fig. 17a   Fig. 17b

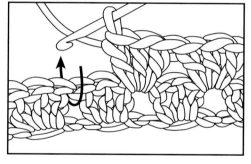

WORKING IN SPACE BEFORE STITCH

When instructed to work in space **before** a stitch or in spaces **between** stitches, insert hook in space indicated by arrow *(Fig. 18)*.

Fig. 18

NO-SEW JOINING

The method used to connect Squares and Flowers is a no-sew joining also known as "join-as-you-go". After the First Square or Flower is made, each remaining Square or Flower is worked to the last rnd, then crocheted together as the last rnd is worked. Holding pieces with **wrong** sides together, work slip st into stitch or space as indicated *(Fig. 19)*.

Fig. 19

FINISHING

WHIPSTITCH

With **wrong** sides together and beginning in corner stitch, sew through both pieces once to secure the beginning of the seam, leaving an ample yarn end to weave in later. Insert needle from **front** to **back** through **inside** loops of **each** piece *(Fig. 20a)* **or** through **both** loops *(Fig. 20b)*. Bring needle around and insert it from **front** to **back** through the next loops of **both** pieces. Continue in this manner across to next corner, keeping the sewing yarn fairly loose.

Fig. 20a

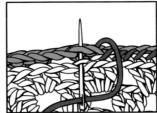

Fig. 20b

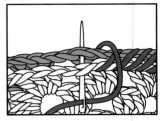

WEAVING

With **right** side of two Panels facing you, bottom edges at same end and edges even, sew through both pieces once to secure the beginning of the seam, leaving an ample yarn end to weave in later. Insert the needle from **right** to **left** through one strand on each piece *(Fig. 21)*. Bring the needle around and insert it from **right** to **left** through the next strand on both pieces. Continue in this manner, drawing seam together as you work.

Fig. 21

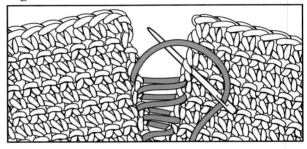

FRINGE

Cut a piece of cardboard 8" wide and $1/2$" longer than desired fringe. Wind the yarn **loosely** and **evenly** around the length of the cardboard until the card is filled, then cut across one end; repeat as needed. Align the number of strands desired and fold in half. With **wrong** side facing and using a crochet hook, draw the folded end up through a stitch, row, or loop, and pull the loose ends through the folded end *(Figs. 22a & b)*; draw the knot up **tightly** *(Figs. 22c & d)*. Repeat, spacing as specified. Lay flat on a hard surface and trim the ends.

Fig. 22a

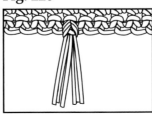

Fig. 22b

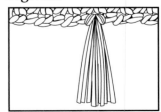

Fig. 22c

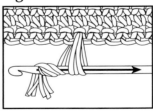

Fig. 22d

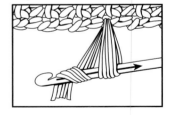

CREDITS

To Magna IV Color Imaging of Little Rock, Arkansas, we say thank you for the superb color reproduction and excellent pre-press preparation.

We want to especially thank photographers Ken West and Mark Mathews of Peerless Photography, Jerry R. Davis of Jerry Davis Photography, and Larry Pennington of Pennington Studios, all of Little Rock, Arkansas, for their time, patience, and excellent work.

We would like to extend a special word of thanks to the talented designers who created the lovely projects in this book:

Eleanor Albano: *Evergreen,* page 126
Carol Alexander: *Classic Aran,* page 102
Carla Bentley: *Bold Plaid,* page 122
Carol Decker: *Dainty Delight,* page 66
Juanita Langham Froese: *Chain of Hearts,* page 128
Nancy Fuller: *Ocean Beauty,* page 50
Cathy Grivnow: *Rosebud,* page 59
Anne Halliday: *Tranquillity,* page 10; *Garden of Flowers,* page 19; *Blue Delft,* page 26; *A Pretty Welcome,* page 28; *Nighty-Night Granny,* page 37; *Ladybugs,* page 53; *Diamond Ripple,* page 62; *Dazzling Diamonds,* page 71; *Breezy Stripes,* page 80; *Dignified,* page 96; *Focal Point,* page 99; *Ski Lodge,* page 114; and *Stunning,* page 118
Jan Hatfield: *Dashing Throw,* page 124
Terry Kimbrough: *Vintage Lace,* page 8; *Story Time,* page 32; and *Double Cozy,* page 130
Tammy Kreimeyer: *Honeycomb,* page 78; *Luxurious Wrap,* page 92; and *Twilight Snowflakes,* page 132
Cynthia Lark: *Fall Portrait,* page 86
Melissa Leapman: *Gentle Raindrops,* page 6; *Summer Mint,* page 42; *Patriotic Starburst,* page 46; *Toasty Earth Tones,* page 84; *Harvest Appeal,* page 88; *Cozy Checks,* page 110; *Winter Abloom,* page 112; *Winter Warmer,* page 116; and *Christmas Cover-up,* page 120
Carole Prior: *Sunrise Ripple,* page 44; *Floral Comfort,* page 64; *Golden Harvest,* page 82; *Radiant Ripples,* page 90; *Ablaze With Color,* page 94; and *Frosty Windows,* page 108
Rhonda Semonis: *Summer Lace,* page 48
Mary Ann Sipes: *Around the Block,* page 16
Maggie Weldon: *Glorious Lilacs,* page 12; *Southern Blossoms,* page 14; *Forget-Me-Not Bouquet,* page 34; and *Morning Glory,* page 68
Betty Wells: *Lovely Look,* page 56
Carole G. Wilder: *Timeless Favorite,* page 76
Patricia Zihala: *Bunny Love,* page 22